Dr. Walter J. Urban's
POWERFUL POEMS

85 YEARS OLD

EIGHTY FIVE YEARS OLD
WATCHING LIFE UNFOLD
I HAVE LEARNED TO SAY
EVERY SINGLE DAY
THE BEST WAY TO START
WITH LOVE IN MY HEART

2017

I AM LIGHT ENERGY PEACE LOVE AND GRATEFUL.

authorHOUSE®

AuthorHouse™
1663 Liberty Drive
Bloomington, IN 47403
www.authorhouse.com
Phone: 1 (800) 839-8640

Published by AuthorHouse 09/26/2017

ISBN: 978-1-5462-0913-3 (sc)
ISBN: 978-1-5462-0912-6 (e)

This book of poems is dedicated to the hope that Humanity wakes up and takes the necessary actions before it destroys Itself and the Planet.

Thanks to my loving wife Fraida who I love with all my heart.

Contents

A

B

C

H

K

L

M

N

U

V

W

Y

Why so many poems?

Poems are a concise way to express our thought
and maybe stimulate the mind to think.

Thoughts are Energy which is the potential for Action.

People seek happiness because they don't have it.
To have Happiness in our society, Health, Love & Money
seem to be prerequisites for many.

Seeking what you do not have can prevent happiness.
Appreciating what you have facilitates happiness.

If you learn how to open your mind
you can receive, learn, change and improve.
You are your greatest asset
and self-development is your choice.

Automatically repeating your past thoughts,
ideas, emotions, behavior, actions, defenses, etc.,
will kept you where you are.

Develop the discipline you need to do what you want in your life.
Prevent parts of your past from becoming your future
and create your new Destiny.
The Choice is yours.

I send all of you my Love
and hope you receive it.

-Walter, September 2016

MY LOVE IS FREE
A GIFT FROM ME
SO CATCH THE VIBE
AND JOIN LOVE'S TRIBE

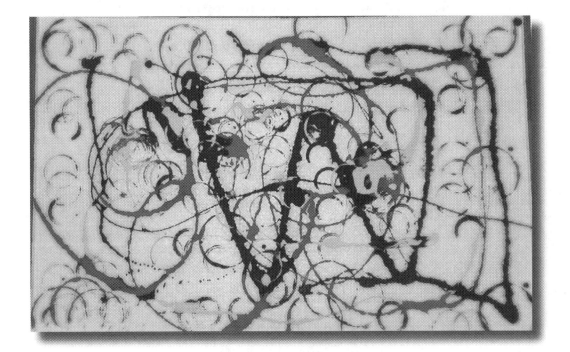

NEW PATH TO TAKE
GET RID OF STRIFE
START A NEW LIFE

A BIRD'S SONG

A BIRD'S SONG
NEVER LONG
NATURE'S CALL
WINTER FALL
LISTEN CLEAR
YOU WILL HEAR
SOUNDS SO TRUE
LOVING YOU
ALL SWEET SOUNDS
YOU SURROUNDS
HEAR THE LIGHT
NATURE'S RIGHT
NEVER LONG
A BIRDS SONG

ACCEPT LIFE

ACCEPT YOUR LIFE
GET RID OF STRIFE
GIVE UP YOUR PAIN
AND DON'T COMPLAIN
BECAUSE YOU KNOW
YOUR WAY TO GO
SO UNDERSTAND
IT'S IN YOUR HAND
WHAT YOU WILL DO
IT'S UP TO YOU
YOUR PATH YOU CHOOSE
DON'T CRY THE BLUES
LEARN YOUR NEW WAY
PRACTICE EACH DAY
DECISION MAKE

A DAY

EACH MORNING WHEN I AWAKE
A NEW DEEP BREATH I WILL TAKE
I'LL THINK OF THE DAY
AND BE ON MY WAY
THE FIRST THING I WILL DO
WILL BE TO THINK OF YOU
THEN I START MY ROUTINE
OF KEEPING MYSELF CLEAN
THE DAY HAS MANY THINGS
BUT FIRST THE BIRD SINGS
A BEAUTIFUL SONG OF LOVE
AND OF THE HEAVEN ABOVE
IF I KEEP THIS IN MIND
THEN GOOD LUCK WILL I FIND
AND ALL THROUGH THE DAY
THINGS WILL GO MY WAY

A FRIEND

EVER HAVE A FRIEND
WITH YOU TO THE END
SUCH A RARE FIND
ONE OF A KIND
SOMEONE YOU CAN TRUST
IF YOU SHOULD GO BUST
ALWAYS THERE FOR YOU
KNOWING WHAT TO DO
WHEN YOU ARE IN NEED
YOU DON'T HAVE TO PLEAD
YOU DON'T HAVE TO ASK
FRIEND WILL DO THE TASK
HOW LUCKY YOU ARE

DON'T HAVE TO GO FAR
YOUR FRIEND IS SO NEAR
AND ALWAYS WILL HEAR
THINGS YOU HAVE TO SAY
EVERY SINGLE DAY
EVER HAVE A FRIEND
WITH YOU TO THE END

A FRIEND (2)

DO YOU HAVE A FRIEND
WHO'LL STAY TILL THE END
IF YOU THINK YOU DO
AND YOUR FRIEND IS TRUE
HOW LUCKY YOU ARE
HAVING SUCH A STAR
THAT SHINES IN THE NIGHT
ALWAYS IN YOUR SIGHT
WILL ALWAYS BE THERE
AND NO MATTER WHERE
YOU DECIDE TO GO
IT WILL ALWAYS SHOW
SO HIGH IN THE SKY
MAKES YOU WONDER WHY
THAT GOD HAS SEND
YOUR TRUE FRIEND

A HUNDRED
YEARS OLD

A HUNDRED YEARS OLD
STORY TO BE TOLD
A HUNDRED ONE
TIME TO HAVE FUN
A HUNDRED TWO
IS GOOD FOR YOU
A HUNDRED THREE
IS GOOD FOR ME

A HUNDRED FOUR
OPEN NEW DOOR
A HUNDRED FIVE
YES STILL ALIVE
A HUNDRED SIX
LEARNING NEW TRICKS
HUNDRED SEVEN
CAN SEE HEAVEN
A HUNDRED EIGHT
CAN SEE THE GATE
A HUNDRED NINE
A CUP OF WINE
A HUNDRED TEN
WILL START AGAIN

A LITTLE LOVE

A LITTLE LOVE MAKES YOU FEEL
THAT YOUR SOUL YOU WILL REVEAL
YOU'LL OPEN YOUR HEART
AND GET A FRESH START
AFTER THOSE YEARS OF PAIN
THE LOVE THAT WAS IN VAIN
ALWAYS BELIEVING
LOVE WAS CONCEIVING
THAT YOU COULD LIVE AGAIN
KNOWING THAT SOMEDAY WHEN
YOU WOULD FIND
LOVE IN MIND
KNOWING NOT WHERE
YOU TOOK A DARE
AND DREAMED FOR THE DAY
LOVE TO COME YOUR WAY
SO HERE YOU ARE
NOT VERY FAR
YOUR DREAM IS REAL
HOW GREAT YOU FEEL
A LITTLE LOVE CAME YOUR WAY
KNOWING HERE YOUR HEART WILL STAY

ADDICTION

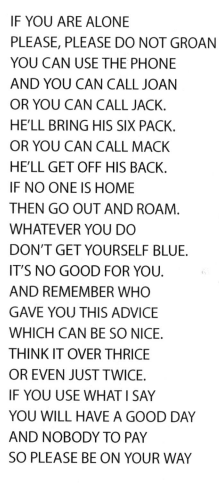

YOUR ADDICTION
YOUR RESTRICTION
YOU BUY MORE THINGS
A TOY THAT SINGS
MORE MORE AND MORE
IN EVERY STORE
YOU WANT IT ALL
AND THEN YOU FALL
OPEN YOUR EYES
AND BECOME WISE
DON'T BE A SLAVE
OR A DUMB KNAVE
SAVE YOUR MONEY
LOVE YOUR HONEY
YOUR ADDICTION
YOUR RESTRICTION

ALERT MIND

KEEP YOUR MIND ALERT
THEN YOU WON'T BE HURT
IF YOU LET IT SLIP
YOU'LL SUFFER THE WHIP
CAUTION IS NEEDED
THE GROUND WELL SEEDED
WITH ALL GOOD SEEDS
HONESTY LEADS
AND SHOWS THE WAY
THE PLACE TO STAY
HARMONY WITH EARTH
GIVING A NEW BIRTH
TO MANKIND AND LOVE
STOP THE PUSH AND SHOVE
WALK ARM IN ARM
MOUNTAIN AND FARM
LOVING THE RAIN
FREEING THE PAIN

FEELING THE JOY
LIKE A CHILD'S TOY
PLAYING WITH DIRT
STOPPING TO FLIRT
BREATHING ALL THE WAY
ON EARTH HERE TO STAY

ALONE

IF YOU ARE ALONE
PLEASE, PLEASE DO NOT GROAN
YOU CAN USE THE PHONE
AND YOU CAN CALL JOAN
OR YOU CAN CALL JACK.
HE'LL BRING HIS SIX PACK.
OR YOU CAN CALL MACK
HE'LL GET OFF HIS BACK.
IF NO ONE IS HOME
THEN GO OUT AND ROAM.
WHATEVER YOU DO
DON'T GET YOURSELF BLUE.
IT'S NO GOOD FOR YOU.
AND REMEMBER WHO
GAVE YOU THIS ADVICE
WHICH CAN BE SO NICE.
THINK IT OVER THRICE
OR EVEN JUST TWICE.
IF YOU USE WHAT I SAY
YOU WILL HAVE A GOOD DAY
AND NOBODY TO PAY
SO PLEASE BE ON YOUR WAY

ALONE

I AM ALONE
I AM UNKNOWN
I DO NOT GROAN
WITHOUT CELL PHONE

AND WHERE ARE YOU
WHAT DO YOU DO
WHAT DO YOU SAY
EVERY NEW DAY
WHAT DO YOU THINK
WHERE IS THE LINK
TO YOUR OWN HEART
THE PLACE TO START
CAN YOU BE BRAVE
AND NOT A SLAVE
GIVE IT A TRY
AND WONDER WHY
YOU WAIT TILL NOW
TO NATURE BOW
SO TIME HAS COME
ONLY FOR SOME
GET THE IDEA
LET GO OF FEAR
I DO NOT MIND
I AM NOT BLIND
I AM ALONE
I AM UNKNOWN

ALONE (2)

YOU'RE NEVER ALONE
YOU DON'T NEED THE PHONE
CAUSE YOU HAVE THE SKY
AND GOD'S WATCHING EYE
YOU HAVE THE MOUNTAINS TOO
AND THE OCEANS SO BLUE
RIVERS AND STREAMS
AND THE SUN'S BEAMS
YOU HAVE THE STARS
AND EVEN MARS
DON'T FORGET THE TREES
AND THEIR MILLION LEAVES
YOU HAVE THE DAY AND NIGHT
TUCKED UNDER COVERS TIGHT
SO WHEN YOU GO TO SLEEP

YOU DON'T HAVE TO COUNT SHEEP
THINK OF ALL THESE THINGS
PRINCES, QUEENS AND KINGS
ARE ALL THERE FOR YOU
AND REMEMBER WHO
YOU'RE NEVER ALONE
YOU DON'T NEED THE PHONE

ALONE (3)

ALONE AT MY AGE
LIFE IS JUST A STAGE
TEARS RUNNING DOWN MY CHEEK
IT BEEN OVER A WEEK
THAT I'VE CRIED AND CRIED
AND I'VE SIGHED AND SIGHED
FEELING ALL MY PAIN
WAITING FOR MY GAIN
NOW THAT I KNOW
WHERE I MUST GO
AWAY FORM POLLUTION
FINDING MY SOLUTION
SO I CAN START ANEW
FINDING LOVE THROUGH AND THROUGH
THE LOVE I NEVER HAD
WHICH MADE ME FEEL SO SAD
THAT BROUGHT ON THE TEARS
THAT GAVE ME THE FEARS
LEARNED THE LESSONS OF LIFE
CUTTING LIKE A SHARP KNIFE
THROUGH MY BEING
WITHOUT SEEING
TEACHING ME TO SMILE
RUNNING THE LAST MILE
NO LONGER ALONE
I'LL GET A CELLPHONE

ALL ABOUT LOVE

IT'S ALL ABOUT LOVE
GUIDANCE FROM ABOVE
ALWAYS TOUCHING YOUR HEART
ALWAYS WITH A FRESH START
SO LOVE NEVER DIES
FOR THOSE WHO ARE WISE
HEART OPEN AND WARM
ALWAYS TRUE TO FORM
FORMS TEARS IN YOU EYES
WITH OPEN MOUTH SIGNS
AS THEY ROLL DOWN YOUR CHEEK
YOUR TRUE LOVE YOU WILL SEEK
AND HOPE THAT YOU FIND
THAT SPECIAL RIGHT KIND
OF LOVE THAT YOU KNOW
THAT WILL ALWAYS GROW
AS YOUR TEARS MULTIPLY
YOU ALWAYS WONDER WHY
YOU CHOKE YOUR TEARS AGAIN
ALWAYS WONDERING WHEN
YOU WILL FIND YOUR WAY
LOVE IS HERE TO STAY
YES ITS ALL ABOUT LOVE
WITH GUIDANCE FROM ABOVE

ALL THIS LOVE

ALL THIS LOVE TO GIVE
HOW I WANT TO LIVE
WITH SOMEONE LIKE YOU
SO I WON'T BE BLUE
HEART IS FILLED WITH LOVE
GOODNESS FROM ABOVE
HERE I AM ALONE
WITH THE USELESS PHONE
NO ONE IS THERE
WITH WHOM TO SHARE

SO WHAT DO I DO
KEEP THINKING OF YOU
AND WAIT FOR THE DAY
WHEN YOU COME MY WAY
THEN YOU WILL SEE
THE LOVE IN ME
ALL THIS LOVE TO GIVE
HOW I WANT TO LIVE

ASK GOD

EVERY SINGLE DAY
I ASK GOD THE WAY
HE SAYS TO ME
LEARN TO BE FREE
YOU NEED NOT ASK
ITS YOUR TASK
KEEP TRAVELING AND UNRAVELING
YOU WILL FIND, EVERY KIND
OF FEELING, YOU'RE REVEALING
BECAUSE YOU KNOW, IT WILL SHOW
THE KIND OF BEING, WITH YOUR SEEING
THAT EACH DAY COMES AND GOES
AND THAT NOBODY KNOWS
WHAT TOMORROW WILL BRING
AND IF THE BIRDS WILL SING
SO WHEN YOU ASK GOD THE WAY
YOU CAN BE SURE HE WILL SAY
HAVE A HAPPY DAY

AVERAGE AMERICAN

I AM A SLAVE
AND I BEHAVE
I AM A FOOL
I FOLLOW THE RULE
DO WHAT I'M TOLD
UNTIL I'M OLD

I HAVE NO CHOICE
I HAVE NO VOICE
MY BRAIN YOU KEEP
I AM ASLEEP
YOU OWN MY MIND
TRUTH I CAN'T FIND
I'M SO CONFUSED
I HAVE BEEN USED
I AM A SLAVE
AND I BEHAVE

AWAKEN

GET AWAKE
FOR YOUR SAKE
DOUBLE TAKE
THEN YOU MAKE
A CLEAR PLAN
BEST YOU CAN
FIND YOUR WAY
EVERYDAY
WORLD UPSET
BUT DON'T FRET
YOU'RE ALIVE
AND WILL THRIVE
FOR YOUR SAKE
GET AWAKE

AWAKEN (2)

HEAR THE SPIRIT
LISTEN AND HEAR IT
IT'S ALL AROUND
IT MAKES NO SOUND
YOUR HEART HAS EYES
IT IS SO WISE
INFINITY
SERENITY
THERE WE ALL GO
END OF THE SHOW

AWAKENING

AS YOU WAKE UP
COMES THE SHAKE UP
OPEN THE EYES
KNOW THE LIES
TRUTH EMERGING
PASSION SURGING
TAKING THESE YEARS
MUCH BLOOD AND TEARS
TO UNDERSTAND
ILLUSION GRAND
OH WHAT GREAT FOOLS
MEDIA TOOLS
LOSING POWER
CONSCIOUS SHOWER
AND BIT BY BIT
AND THERE YOU SIT
SWALLOWING IT
A LOAD OF SHIT
FINALLY LIGHT
IN THE DARK NIGHT
NOW YOU GET IT
YES I'VE SAID IT
INNER STRENGTH GROWS
FROM HEAD TO TOES

YOU LOST YOUR FEAR
YOUR LIFE IS DEAR
AND SO YOU CHOOSE
NEVER TO LOSE
AS YOU WAKE UP
COMES THE SHAKE UP

ANSWERS?

COMPLICATED PHILOSOPHIES AND GREAT
    RELIGIONS
MAY NOT BE THE ANSWER TO SIMPLE LIVING
    AND GIVING
SO WHAT DO WE NEED TO LEARN
WHICH WAY DO WE TURN
DO WE NEED CLASSES
TO LOOK AT SHAPELY ASSES
OR A MUSCLE MAN
WITH A NICE TAN
NATURE IS OUR TEACHER
DO WE NEED A PREACHER
WHY COMPLICATE LIFE
AND ADD SO MUCH STRIFE
WHERE ARE YOU GOING
IS YOUR HEART SHOWING
AND DO YOU FEEL THE LOVE
OR SEE THE SKY ABOVE
DO YOU HAVE THE PEACE
AND YOUR STRESS DOES CEASE
DRAW YOUR CONCLUSION
NO MORE ILLUSION
IS THIS OK TO SEND OUT TO PEOPLE
OR SHALL I HIDE THIS IN A STEEPLE?

B

BE ALONE

BE ALONE
NO CELL PHONE
DON'T USE FAX
YOU RELAX
FIND YOUR PEACE
LIFE'S NEW LEASE
TRY IT NOW
TO NATURE BOW
YOU WILL LEARN
IN GOOD TURN
HOW TO DO
WHAT IS NEW
NO CELL PHONE
BE ALONE

BEAUTIFUL WORLD

DEATH UNFURLED
EMBRYO CURLED
WHY CAN'T YOU SEE
IT SHOULD NOT BE
POWER CONTROL
IT'S NOT YOUR ROLE
SO CHANGE YOUR MIND
LOVE HEART AND KIND
LEARN UNDERSTAND
YOU'RE NOT SO GRAND
LOOK AT A TREE
WALK TO THE SEA
REMEMBER LOVE
THE STARS ABOVE
STOP YOUR KILLING

WHY SO WILLING
YOU ARE POSSESSED
YOU ARE OBSESSED
CORPORATIONS
ONE WORLD NATIONS
SUCH DESTRUCTION
NEED CONSTRUCTION
BEAUTIFUL WORLD
EMBRYO CURLED

BEAUTY EYES

BEAUTY EYES
LOVELY THIGHS
GREAT BIG SIGHS
HEAD SO WISE
HEART SO WARM
WHAT A FORM
HEART SO TRUE
I LOVE YOU
EVERY DAY
EVERY WAY
WITH YOUR SMILE
YOU BEGUILE
LOVELY THIGHS
BEAUTY EYES

BECOME AWARE

BECOME AWARE
NOT A BLIND STARE
IF YOU STAY ASLEEP
AND COUNT MORE SHEEP
YOU'LL HAVE SURPRISE
BELIEVING LIES
THAT OWN YOUR LIFE
HUSBAND AND WIFE
CHILDREN PREPARE

AND TAKE THE DARE
AND OPEN YOUR EYES
AND BECOME WISE
AND PLANT YOUR FOOD
GET IN THE MOOD
PROTECT YOUR LIFE
FROM GLOBAL STRIFE
DO IT TODAY
AND DON'T DELAY
SEE THE LIGHT GLARE
BECOME AWARE

HOPING I'LL GET SOME BRAKES
NOW I WILL CLOSE MY EYES
AND I SEE THE BLUE SKIES
AND ALL THE STARS
AND EVEN MARS
BEFORE I KNOW IT
MY FACE WILL SHOW IT
I AM SOUND ASLEEP
NOT A SINGLE PEEP
WHEN I GO TO BED
AND LAY DOWN MY HEAD

BED TIME

WHEN I WENT TO BED
GOD WAS IN MY HEAD
IT WAS A GOOD THOUGHT
A LESSON GOD TAUGHT.
I KNEW I WOULD SLEEP SO WELL
FOR GOD DID TELL
HOPING FOR A HAPPY WORD
FROM GOD IT WAS HEARD
SO NOW I KNOW WHERE TO GO
GOD DOES ALWAYS SHOW
BEST WAY TO DO THE THINGS
IS FLYING ON GOD'S WINGS

BELIEFS

WHAT YOU BELIEVE
HOW YOU DECEIVE
YOUR OWN BEING
WITHOUT SEEING
YOU STOP THE FLOW
OF WHERE YOU GO
YOU LOOSE YOUR CHOICE
GIVE UP YOUR VOICE
SO TAKE A LOOK
PUT DOWN THE BOOK
THAT MAKES THE RULES
CONTROLS THE FOOLS
LET IT ALL GO
AND WATCH THE SHOW
AND DON'T DECEIVE
WHAT YOU BELIEVE

BED TIME (2)

WHEN I GO TO BED
AND LAY DOWN MY HEAD
I REVIEW MY DAY
DID THINGS GO MY WAY
WHAT WILL I DO TOMORROW
I WILL HAVE JOY NOT SORROW
ALL THE THINGS I WILL DO
I'LL WORK TILL I AM THROUGH
NO MATTER WHAT IT TAKES

BELIEVING

I AM NEVER ALONE
I DON'T NEED A CELL PHONE
ALWAYS WITH YOU
WHATEVER I DO
ALWAYS IN MY MIND

SO LOVING AND KIND
WE ARE PART OF EACH OTHER
LIKE BABY AND ITS MOTHER
LONG AS I BELIEVE
YOU WILL NOT DECEIVE
YOU HAVE MANY NAMES
FOR THOSE WHO PLAY GAMES
YOU ARE ONLY ONE
LIKE THE GIANT SUN
THAT KEEPS US ALIVE
SO ALL CAN SURVIVE
WE NEED YOU FOR LIFE
LIKE HUSBAND NEEDS WIFE
SO I SAY THIS TO YOU
I WILL ALWAYS BE TRUE
YOU ARE MY GOD FOREVER
MY LIFE'S GREATEST ENDEAVOR

BE LIKE

BE LIKE A BIRD FREE
BE LIKE A LION STRONG
BE LIKE A DOG LOYAL
BE LIKE A BEE PRODUCTIVE
BE LIKE A TREE SILENT
BE LIKE A WOMAN CARING
BE LIKE A MAN LOGICAL
BE LIKE AN ANT ORGANIZED
BE LIKE A CAT CONTENTED
BE LIKE A MONKEY VERSATILE
BE LIKE AN EAGLE SEEING
BE LIKE A TIGER READY
BE LIKE A STAR GLOWING
BE LIKE A SUN GIVING
BE LIKE A RIVER FLOWING
BE LIKE A FLOWER SWEET
BE LIKE A CHILD CURIOUS
BE LIKE A BEAR REST
BE LIKE AN ARTIST CREATIVE
BE LIKE A YOGI FLEXIBLE

BE LIKE A MONK SELF CONTAINED
BE LIKE A WARRIOR COURAGEOUS
BE LIKE THE DAY BRIGHT
BE LIKE YOURSELF ORIGINAL
BE LIKE LOVE FORGIVING
BE LIKE JOY SHARING
BE LIKE THE HEART WISE
BE LIKE THE BRAIN THINKING
BE LIKE THE STOMACH DIGESTING
BE LIKE WHATEVER YOU WANT TO BE

BEYOND SPIRIT

BEYOND SPIRIT
LISTEN HEAR IT
THE GREAT UNKNOWN
NEW SEEDS ARE GROWN
MYSTICS ALIVE
BEYOND THE JIVE
NOTHING TO SELL
KEEP YOURSELF WELL
NO GURU LIES
NO MONEY TIES
ITS ALL SO FREE
THE WAY TO BE
SEARCH AND THEN FIND
PEACE IN YOUR MIND
LISTEN HEAR IT
BEYOND SPIRIT

BIG STAR

OH BIG STAR
GREAT YOU ARE
UP SO HIGH
IN THE SKY
SHINE SO BRIGHT
ALL THE NIGHT

THEN YOU GO
NO MORE SHOW
TILL NEXT DAY
THAT'S YOUR WAY
COME THE DARK
SEE YOUR SPARK
GREAT YOU ARE
MY BIG STAR

BIG TREE

GREAT BIG TREE
I LOVE THEE
WITH DEEP ROOTS
AND NEW SHOOTS
HOME TO ALL
HEAR BIRDS CALL
WATER AND AIR
EVERYWHERE
SUN BEAMS STRONG
TREE LIVES LONG
WITHSTANDS TIME
LIKE THIS RHYME
I LOVE THEE
GREAT BIG TREE

BLEEDING EYES, CRYING HEART

BLEEDING EYES, CRYING HEART
HOPING FOR A NEW START
FOR LOVE TO COME MY WAY
BEGINNING EVERY DAY
AWAY FROM THE MATERIAL SIDE
WITH MY EYES NOW OPEN VERY WIDE
I LOOK AND WHAT DO I SEE
AN OLDER PICTURE OF ME
AS THE DAYS GO BY

I BECOME LESS SHY
THEN I HOPE FOR LOVE
LIKE A TURTLE DOVE
IN THE SKY
FLYING HIGH
CLOSER TO THE SUN
WHERE LIFE HAS BEGUN
WHERE LIFE FLOURISHES
AND HEART NOURISHES
NO MORE CRYING
NO MORE SIGHING
THEN THE EYES ARE CLEAR
I FOUND YOU MY DEAR
IN MY DREAMS
SO IT SEEMS
WAITING TO BE REAL
WHEN LIFE I CAN FEEL
BLEEDING EYES, CRYING HEART
HOPING FOR A NEW START

BLUE SKY

WHITE CLOUDS BLUE SKY
I WONDER WHY
GREEN GRASS BIG TREES
FALLING BROWN LEAVES
TURNING TO DUST
LOSING ALL LUST
AND THEN REBORN
FROM THE BREAST TORN
AND THEN REGROW
START A NEW SHOW
BEARING NEW FRUIT
LOOKING SO CUTE
NEW STRENGTH TO START
WITH OPEN HEART
I WONDER WHY
WHITE CLOUDS BLUE SKY

BRAIN AND HEART

BRAIN THINKS SO MUCH
HEART LOVES TO TOUCH
BRAIN LIVES IN FEAR
HEART LOVES YOU DEAR
WHICH DO YOU CHOOSE
WANT TO WIN OR LOSE
BRAIN CRIES IN PAIN
LOVE IS TO GAIN
SO STOP AND THINK
DON'T LET HEART SINK
FOR IF YOU DO
IT'S YOU YOU SCREW
BRAIN THINKS TO MUCH
LOVE LOVES TO TOUCH

BUSY

SO SO BUSY
ALMOST DIZZY
NEED SOME MORE
THE WHOLE STORE
BUY BUY BUY
WONDER WHY
LOVE NEW TOYS
BRINGS NEW JOYS
MY SPIRIT
WHERE IS IT
LOOK AROUND
CAN'T BE FOUND
WHAT TO DO
TO BE TRUE

SHOW THE WAY
EVERY DAY
HELPING FRIENDS
TO GOOD ENDS
HAVE NO TIME
END THE RHYME
VERY BUSY
VERY DIZZY

BY MY SIDE

BY MY SIDE
LOVE DOES RIDE
FAR AND WIDE
THEN DOES HIDE
THEN RETURNS
WITH ITS BURNS
FIRE STRONG
LASTS SO LONG
LOVELY DAYS
ALL THE WAYS
FINDING WHERE
IN LOVE'S STARE
LOVE DOES RIDE
BY MY SIDE

CALM

MAINTAIN YOUR CALM
THERE'S NO ALARM
RELAX YOUR HEART
IT'S THERE YOU START
AND THEN YOUR MIND
LEARN TO BE KIND
AND SO IT GOES
FROM HEAD TO TOES
LEARNING THE WAY
TO LIVE EACH DAY
WATER FLOWING
WITH LOVE GROWING
LIKE A NEW SEED
SPROUTING YOUR CREED
THERE'S NO ALARM
MAINTAIN YOUR CALM

CAN'T THE WORLD
EVER HAVE PEACE?

CAN'T THE WORLD EVER HAVE PEACE?
I CRY FOR THE WORLD
WHEN I THINK, ABOUT IT
I CRY EVERY DAY
I WISH THERE WAS ANOTHER WAY
WHEN WILL LOVE'S BANNER BE UNFURLED
SO HERE I SIT
IN MY CHAIR AT HOME
MY HEART DOES ROAM
MY MIND SEES IT ALL
THE RISE AND THE FALL

IT IS SO COMPLICATED
THAT MAN'S HISTORY IS SO HARD
THAT DREAMS ARE UNABATED
THOUGH LOVE HAS BEEN CREATED
AND HAS NOT YET BEEN BARRED
FROM ENTERING HIS MIND
HE IS ABLE TO FIND
A WAY THROUGH ALL THIS
AND NOT GO AMISS
CAN'T THE WORLD EVER HAVE PEACE
AND GREED, CORRUPTION AND VIOLENCE
    CEASE
I SIT HERE ALL ALONE
AS IF MY CHAIR WAS MY THRONE
AND WONDER WHAT HAS GONE WRONG
EVENT THOUGH WE SING GOD'S SONG
IT GOES ON AND ON AND STAYS THE SAME
IS MAN'S SPIRIT IN GOD'S NAME?
I CRY FOR THE WORLD!
CAN'T THE WORLD EVER HAVE PEACE?

CAN'T YOU SEE

CAN'T YOU SEE
YOU'RE NOT FREE
YOU'RE A SLAVE
TO THE GRAVE
THEY OWN YOU
AND ME TOO
YOU OBEY
EVERY DAY
IF YOU DON'T
AND YOU WON'T
LIFE YOU LOOSE
SO YOU CHOOSE
SELL YOUR SOUL
IT'S THEIR GOAL
CAN'T YOU SEE
YOU'RE NOT FREE

CELL PHONE

CELL PHONE WORLD
CONTROL UNFURLED
RADIATION
THROUGH THE NATION
THE MIND CONTROLLED
SLOW DEATH UNROLLED
ADDICTION FORMED
FACEBOOK IS STORMED
TV REPLACED
HUMANS DISGRACED
NO LONGER THINKS
THE WHOLE THING STINKS
THE PLANET SINKS
BOTH EYES HAVE BLINKS
AND CANNOT SEE
HUMANITY
CONTROL UNFURLED
THE CELL PHONE WORLD

CELL PHONE (2)

LEAVE ME ALONE
SHUT MY CELL PHONE
PLEASE NO MORE CALLS
I BUILD THE WALLS
I NEED SOME SPACE
GET OUT OF RACE
I AM TIRED
GET ME FIRED
PLEASE NO MORE JOB
I'M JUST POOR SLOB
I WANT TO HIDE
I HAVE MY PRIDE
CAN'T PAY MY BILLS
AND NO MORE THRILLS
JUST LET ME BE
FOR CAN'T YOU SEE

I AM TOO CONFUSED
AND OVER USED
LEAVE ME ALONE
NO MORE CELL PHONE

CHANGE

CORRUPTION
ERUPTION
HERE AND THERE
EVERYWHERE
MUCH KILLING
SO WILLING
ENDLESS CRIME
A SAD TIME
WAR AND BOMBS
DESTROY FARMS
CHILDREN DIE
MOTHERS CRY
AWAKE MIND
PEACE YOU FIND

CHANGING

HOW BIG IS YOUR HOUSE
HOW NICE IS YOUR SPOUSE
LOOKING ON THE OUTSIDE
WHEN GOD IS NOT YOUR GUIDE
WHAT KIND OF CAR DO YOU DRIVE
BE GLAD THAT YOU ARE ALIVE
ASK YOURSELF HOW YOU THINK
THEN DISCOVER THE LINK
TO SPIRIT AND LOVE
TO THE SKY ABOVE
YOU'LL OPEN YOUR MIND
BECOME WARM AND KIND
LOOKING INSIDE YOURSELF
YOU'LL FIND THE MAGIC ELF

16

TO HELP YOU ON YOUR WAY
TO HELP YOU LEARN TO PRAY
YOU WON'T NEED ANY MORE
TO OPEN THE NEW DOOR
WHEN YOU ENTER INSIDE
YOU WILL HAVE A NEW PRIDE
YOU WON'T NEED MANY THINGS
TO FLY ON YOUR GOD'S WINGS

CHASING MONEY

CHASING MONEY
IT'S NOT FUNNY
DO ALL YOU CAN
OH HOW THEY RAN
LOOKED EVERYWHERE
IN A BLIND STARE
SEARCHING HIGH LOW
NO WHERE TO GO
RAINBOWS SO BRIGHT
DAY AND ALL NIGHT
UNTIL YOU FIND
YOUR PEACE OF MIND
IT'S NOT FUNNY
CHASING MONEY

CHASING YOUR DREAM

CHASING YOUR DREAM
SO DOES IT SEEM
THAT YOU WILL FIND
YOUR PEACE OF MIND
CHANCES ARE NOT
THIS LIFE YOU GOT
TO FIND ANSWERS
WATCH THE DANCERS
THEY SPIN YOU KNOW

AROUND THEY GO
ALL END THE SAME
NO DREAM NO PAIN
SO LET IT GO
LIVE YOUR OWN SHOW
SO DOES IT SEEM
CHASING YOUR DREAM

CHOICE

YOU HAVE A CHOICE
YOU HAVE A VOICE
AND YOU CAN THINK
QUICK AS A WINK
TO USE YOUR MIND
HOPING TO FIND
THE END TO FEAR
HAVE YOUR MIND CLEAR
AND THEN BE FREE
AND LEARN TO SEE
REALITY
FOR YOU AND ME
YOUR WORLD OF DREAMS
AND SO IT SEEMS
YOU HAVE A VOICE
YOU HAVE A CHOICE

CHOOSE THE WAY

DARK OR LIGHT
DAY OR NIGHT
RAIN OR DRY
LAUGH OR SIGH
UP OR DOWN
SMILE OR FROWN
BACK OR FRONT
PLANT OR HUNT
DO IT ALL

HEAR THE CALL
FREEDOM REIGN
GIVE UP PAIN
CHOOSE THE WAY
EVERYDAY

CLARITY

IT'S ALL SO CLEAR
LIVE IN YOUR FEAR
HEAR ALL THE NEWS
THEY TURN THE SCREWS
AND YOU OBEY
WHAT THEY SAY
IT'S FOR GOOD
DO AS YOU SHOULD
AND NEVER THINK
QUICK AS A WINK
YOU LOSE YOUR MIND
THEN NEVER FIND
WHO YOU CAN BE
AND NEVER SEE
SO LIVE IN FEAR
NOTHING IS CLEAR

CLEAN

CLEAN OUT YOUR MIND
AND FREEDOM FIND
THEY TAUGHT YOU LIES
YOU THOUGHT YOU'RE WISE
BUT NOW YOU KNOW
IT WAS A SHOW
YOU SEE CLEARLY
YOU PAID DEARLY
YOU GAVE YOUR LIFE
YOU LIVED IN STRIFE
OBEYED ORDERS

GAVE YOUR DAUGHTERS
AND YOUR SONS TOO
AND EVEN YOU
DID WHAT YOU'RE TOLD
AND BECAME OLD
IT'S NOT TOO LATE
TO CHANGE YOUR FATE
AND FREEDOM FIND
CLEAN OUT YOUR MIND

CLOSED MIND

CLOSED IS YOUR MIND
YOU NEVER FIND
PEACE IN YOUR SOUL
OR YOUR RIGHT ROLE
SEEK ILLUSION
LIVE CONFUSION
YOU CANNOT LEARN
AROUND YOU TURN
YOU WASTE YOUR LIFE
LIVING IN STRIFE
YOU SEEK ANSWERS
INVENT NEW DANCES
YOU BLAME OTHERS
FATHERS MOTHERS
YOU CANNOT AWAKE
CLOSED IS YOUR MIND
WITH A DEEP SIGH
FOR YOUR OWN SAKE
YOU CANNOT FIND
I WONDER WHY
DON'T EVEN TRY
WATCH LIFE GO BY

COME FEEL MY LOVE

COME FEEL MY LOVE
IT FROM ABOVE
SO COME MY DEAR
STAY VERY NEAR
DON'T LEAVE MY SIDE
NO SPACE THAT'S WIDE
SO CLOSE YOU GET
I CAN'T FORGET
THE GREAT FEELING
MY HEART'S REVEALING
SUCH OPEN JOY
FEELING LOVE'S TOY
ONE THAT IS REAL
HOW GREAT I FEEL
ITS FROM ABOVE
THIS GREAT GREAT LOVE

COMMENTARY

WHAT HAS HAPPENED TO MAN'S SOUL?
IS IT DOWN IN THE BLACK HOLE?
MATERIALISM GREED AND CORRUPTION
IN THE WORLD LIKE VOLCANO IN ERUPTION
WE USED TO TRUST EACH OTHER
NOW YOU CAN'T TRUST YOUR BROTHER
WE BECOME MORE ALONE
EVEN WITH THE CELL PHONE
NO PLACE LEFT TO TURN
WHEN CITIES THEY BURN
TO THIS WE MUST ADJUST
IF WE DON'T WE WILL BUST
SO ONWARD WE GO
IT'S ANOTHER SHOW
AS THE WORLD GOES ROUND
WHERE IS THERE LOVE FOUND
IN YOUR HEART YOU PRESERVE
DON'T EVER LOSE YOUR NERVE

AND YOU WILL FIND
SOME PEACE OF MIND
YOU STOP AND CLEAR YOUR HEAD
BEFORE YOU GO TO BED

COMPASSION

DON'T RATION
COMPASSION
GIVE AWAY
EVERYDAY
MORE YOU DO
BEST FOR YOU
WITH EACH DEED
PLANT THE SEED
THUS YOU SOW
LEARN TO GROW
IN NEW WAYS
ALL THE DAYS
DON'T RATION
COMPASSION

CONFIDENCE

IT'S SO GOOD TO KNOW
YOU'RE PART OF THE SHOW
WHERE EVER YOU GO
YOU GO WITH THE FLOW
YOU FEEL GOOD INSIDE
YOU HAVE ALL YOUR PRIDE
PEOPLE KNOW WHO YOU ARE
EVEN WHEN YOU GO FAR
YOU PLAY THE GAME
YOU HAVE SOME FAME
YOU LIKE WHAT YOU DO
IT'S SUITED FOR YOU
SO KEEP ON YOUR WAY
CONTINUE TO PLAY

IT'S TO GOOD TO KNOW
YOU'RE PART OF THE SHOW

CONFLICT

WHAT TO DO
THINK IT THROUGH
CONFUSION
INTRUSION
YOU DECIDE
FORGET PRIDE
CLEAR IN THOUGHT
CAN'T BE BOUGHT
VALUES STRONG
DO NO WRONG
DO WHAT'S RIGHT
NEEDLESS FIGHT
WHAT TO DO
THINK IT THROUGH

CORPORATE SLAVE

GOOD CORPORATE SLAVE
DIGGING YOUR GRAVE
WORK FOR MASTER
MAKE DISASTER
STEP BACK STOP THINK
STAY UP DON'T SINK
BE YOUR OWN BOSS
STRENTHEN YOUR FORCE
STEP BACK AND LOOK
IS BOSS A CROOK
DON'T BE AFRAID
FREEDOM IS MADE
COURAGOUS BE
THEN YOU WILL SEE
YOU'RE DIGGING GRAVE
AS COIRPORAE SLAVE

COOPERATION

COOPERATION
FOR EVERY NATION
CONNECTING THE HEARTS
WITH ALL LOVING PARTS
ONLY THEN WE FIND
OUR GOOD PEACE OF MIND
OUR HEARTS END THE WARS
ON ALL THE WORLD'S SHORE
GROWING FOOD FOR ALL
NO MORE CHILDREN FALL
WE THEN SEE THE LIGHT
IT'S USELESS TO FIGHT
THUS EVERY NATION
COOPERATION

COUNTDOWN BEGINS

COUNTDOWN BEGINS
HERE COMES THE SINS
SOUNDLY YOU SLEEP
HEAR NOT A PEEP
THINGS ARE CHANGING
NEW WARS WAGING
AND NO MORE CASH
DOLLARS ARE TRASH
FOOD DISAPPEARS
YOUR USELESS TEARS
COME MUCH TOO LATE
YOUR EMPTY PLATE
OH WHAT A DREAM
IT ALL DOES SEEM
YET IT'S ALL TRUE
EVEN TO YOU
YOU WONDER WHY
CHEMICAL SKY
YOU FAIL TO SEE
IT'S YOU AND ME

WITH SILENT VOICE
GAVE UP OUR CHOICE
YOU TRY TO HIDE
RUN FAR AND WIDE
OH WHAT GREAT SINS
THE COUNTDOWN BEGINS

COURAGE

COURAGE TO FIND
GREED TO UNWIND
COURAGE TO DO
LIVE BRAVE AND TRUE
FIRE NOT OUT
BY YOUR BIG SHOUT
SO WHAT IS NEXT
DON'T BE PERPLEXED
DO THE THINGS NOW
NOT TO FEAR BOW
UNDERSTAND THIS
AND YOU WON'T MISS
THE TIME TO START
COMES FROM YOUR HEART
GREED TO UNWIND
COURAGE TO FIND

COURAGE

COURAGE NOT FEAR
LOVE NOT A TEAR
YOU CAN BE BRAVE
NOT BE A SLAVE
OPEN YOUR MIND
LOGIC YOU FIND
RESPECT THE TREES
BIRDS AND THE BEES
WORK ON YOUR DREAM
LIKE NEW SUN BEAM

BE FRESH AND LIGHT
ALL DAY ALL NIGHT
KNOW YOUR MOTHER
RESPECT YOUR BROTHER
AND DON'T FORGET
HAVE NO REGRET
YOU DID YOUR BEST
SO TAKE A REST
AND IF YOU THINK
YOU WILL NOT SINK
AND START EACH DAY
WITH FRESH NEW WAY
COURAGE NOT FEAR
LOVE NOT A TEAR

CRYING WORLD

CRY FOR THE WORLD
CONTROL UNFURLED
DON'T LOSE YOUR SOUL
MAINTAIN YOUR GOAL
KEEP YOUR MIND CLEAR
LET GO OF FEAR
MAINTAIN YOUR HEART
THE PLACE TO START
TRY AS THEY MAY
THEY'LL LOSE THE DAY
MONEY CONTROLLED
NEW LIFE UNFOLD
SO FIND YOUR WAY
NEW GAME YOU PLAY
YOU'VE WON AT LAST
FORGET YOUR PAST
CRY FOR THE WORLD
CONTROL UNFURLED

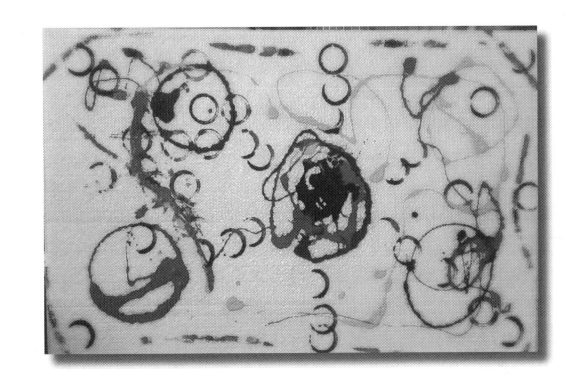

DARK AND LIGHT

LOOK INTO THE DARK
THERE YOU FIND A SPARK
AND SO YOU WILL LEARN
THAT LIGHT HAS ITS TURN
WHEN YOU SEE THE LIGHT
THERE IS NO MORE FIGHT
LIGHT IS YOUR TEACHER
THERE IS NO PREACHER
YOU LEARN FROM YOUR LIFE
GETTING THROUGH YOUR STRIFE
AND THEN YOU ARE FREE
THEN BETTER YOU SEE
THERE IS NO MORE DARK
SEARCH AND FIND YOUR SPARK

DESIRE

SO DOES DESIRE
LIGHT YOUR FIRE
THEN IF IT DOES
YOU GET A BUZZ
YOU'RE ON YOUR WAY
A BUSY DAY
IN FRONT OF YOU
THINK IT THROUGH
BEWARE OF DEEDS
JUST LIKE NEW SEEDS
THEY WILL GROW TALL
AND THEN WILL FALL
ATTENTION PAY
THUS SAVE THE DAY
LIGHT YOUR FIRE
SO GOES DESIRE

DESIRE

YOUR DESIRE
IS BAD FIRE
GET SOME MORE THINGS
BE QUEENS AND KINGS
ACCUMULATE
THAT IS YOUR FATE
FOLLOW THE CROWD
HEAR MUSIC LOUD
OBEY ALL LAWS
DOING YOUR CHORES
KEEP LOOKING GOOD
DO WHAT YOU SHOULD
THE FALSE TEACHERS
THE FALSE PREACHERS
STAY AS A SLAVE
THEN REACH YOUR GRAVE
OR HAVE A CHOICE
EXPRESS YOUR VOICE
STAND UP ALONE
FREE THE CELL PHONE
DROP ALL YOUR FEAR
YOUR HEART STAY NEAR
AND LEARN THE TRUTH
REGAIN YOUR YOUTH
NEVER TOO OLD
OUT OF THE FOLD
LEARN TO BE FREE
FOR CAN'T YOU SEE
YOUR DESIRE
IS BAD FIRE

DO IT

GREAT TEACHER
GREAT PREACHER
WALK THE WALK
STOP THE TALK
DO YOUR BEST
IN LIFE'S TEST
DISCIPLINE
THEN YOU WIN
MORE EACH DAY
IS THE WAY
GET PREPARED
OR BE SAD
NATURE'S CALL
WINS IT ALL

DISCIPLINE

DISCIPLINE LEARN
IT'S NOW YOUR TURN
YOUR TIME TO GROW
LEAVE THE FALSE SHOW
DON'T FOOL YOURSELF
WITH BOOKS ON SHELF
NATURE CONTROLS
YOUR HEARTS AND SOULS
SO SEE THE LIGHT
GIVE UP FALSE FIGHT
FOR WEALTH AND POWER
ENJOY SPRING SHOWER
SEE THE FLOWER
EIFFEL TOWER
SURRENDER NOW
DON'T KILL THE COW
CONTROL YOU MIND
HAPPINESS FIND
IT'S NOW YOUR TURN
DISCIPLINE LEARN

DO IT NOW

DO IT NOW
USE THE PLOW
TIME HAS COME
JUST FOR SOME
GET AWAKE
FOR YOUR SAKE
IT IS LATE
SEAL YOUR FATE
VISION CLEAR
WITHOUT FEAR
WHILE YOU'RE HERE
LOVE MY DEAR
TO NATURE BOW
AND DO IT NOW

DON'T CONTROL

DON'T CONTROL
NOT YOUR ROLE
LET IT BE
THEN CAN SEE
LIGHT IS CLEAR
WITHOUT FEAR
ALL IS HERE
ALL IS NEAR
OPEN YOUR EYES
BECOME WISE
LEARN THE WAY
LIVE THE DAY
NOT YOUR ROLE
TO CONTROL

DO YOU PRAY

EVERYDAY
IF YOU PRAY
YOU WILL SAY
THAT YOU MAY
FIND THE KIND
OF GOOD MIND
SO YOU THINK
QUICK AS WINK
ALL THE THINGS
FEATHERS WINGS
FLYING HIGH
IN BLUE SKY
IF YOU PRAY
EVERYDAY

DREAMING

I'M DREAMING OF YOU
YOU MAKE ME SO BLUE
PLEASE ANSWER YOUR PHONE
I FEEL SO ALONE
THINK OF YOU ALL DAY
LOVE YOU EVERY WAY
SO PLEASE PLEASE AND PLEASE
I'M DOWN ON MY KNEES
I MUST HEAR YOUR VOICE
I DON'T HAVE A CHOICE
YOU MAKE ME SO BLUE
I'M DREAMING OF YOU

DREAMING (2)

EVERYDAY I HAVE A DREAM
I'M RIDING ON A SUNBEAM
I THINK OF ALL NEW THINGS
IF ONLY I HAD WINGS
COME AND GO AS I PLEASE
ENJOY A SUMMER BREEZE
LOOKING AT THE STARS
THE RED PLANET MARS
BUT HERE I AM ON EARTH
GETTING MY MONEY'S WORTH
GOT TO BE REAL
SUFFER AND FEEL
THE JOYS AND PAINS
AND ALL LIFE'S GAINS
THEN I'LL STOP TO THINK
QUICK AS AN EYE BLINK
IT GOES BY SO FAST
HOW LONG WILL LIFE LAST
NO ONE KNOWS
HOW IT GOES
SO WHY NOT DREAM
RIDE A SUNBEAM

DREAMS

ALL THE DREAMS
SO IT SEEMS
ALL DESIRES
ARE YOUR FIRES
SO YOU LIVE
GET AND GIVE
HOPING FOR
OPEN DOOR
FULL OF LIGHT
HUMAN FIGHT
SO WILL END
MESSAGE SEND
SO IT SEEMS
ALL THE DREAMS

DUMB

KEEP PEOPLE DUMB
IT WORKS WITH SOME
IF THEY DON'T KNOW
THE WAY TO GO
THEY'RE LED ASTRAY
AND LOSE THE DAY
FOLLOW WHAT'S TOLD
AND BUY THE GOLD
FOR THOSE AWAKE
NEW PATH WILL TAKE
TRUTH WILL BE FOUND
ON FERTILE GROUND
IF NOT DONE SOON
FLY TO THE MOON
IT WORKS WITH SOME
KEEP PEOPLE DUMB

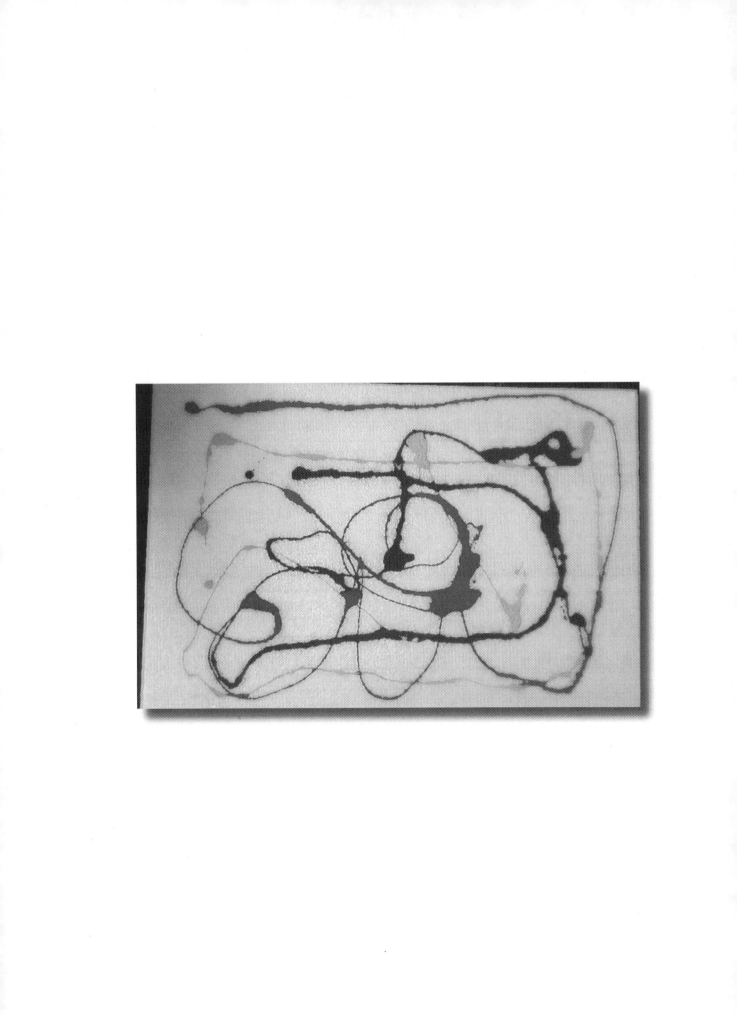

OH HOW THEY GROANED
IT'S EVERYWHERE
EBOLA SCARE

EACH DAY

EACH DAY I PRAY
I CRY I TRY
I WONDER WHY
WISH I COULD FLY
AND SEE BELOW
PLANET'S GREAT SHOW
THE TOPS OF TREES
THE COOLING BREEZE
BUT MOST OF ALL
THE STARS THAT FALL
I SEE MAN'S GREED
THE FARMER'S SEED
AS CHILDREN PLAY
SUNRISE EACH DAY
THE GOOD AND BAD
THE JOY THE SAD
I CRY I TRY
I WONDER WHY

EBOLA WAR

EBOLA WAR
IS AT YOUR DOOR
WE'RE JUST CHECKING
YOUR LIFE WRECKING
YOU TAKE THE TEST
WE'LL DO THE REST
WE HAVE THE CURE
IT IS FOR SURE
JUST TAKE THE SHOT
WOULDN'T FEEL A LOT
SO DON'T REFUSE
LISTEN TO THE NEWS
A MAN HAS DIED
AND WE ALL CRIED
WE'LL SAVE YOUR LIFE
AND END YOUR STRIFE
RIGHT AT YOUR DOOR
EBOLA WAR

EBOLA

EBOLA SCARE
IS EVERYWHERE
WHAT TO BELIEVE
HOW THEY DECEIVE
YOU NEED VACCINE
HOW VERY MEAN
IS IT ALL TRUE
OR JOKE ON YOU
YOU NEVER KNOW
THE TRUTHFUL SHOW
THE NEWS IS OWNED

80 YEARS OLD

BE LIKE ME
AN OLD TREE
BIG AND STRONG
SING A SONG
BE LIKE LOVE
A WHITE DOVE
JOYOUS HEART
IS THE START
THEN REPAIR
EVERYWHERE
START ANEW

SKY SO BLUE
OLD LIKE ME
BE A TREE

82 YEARS OLD

EIGHTY TWO YEARS OLD
MY LIFE WILL UNFOLD
I HAVE SUCH GREAT JOY
THE WORLD IS MY TOY
HAVE SUCH GREAT SPIRIT
THE WORLD CAN HEART IT
AND WOULD LIKE TO SHARE
WITH YOU IF YOU DARE
SO COME JOIN ME NOW
AND TAKE A BIG BOW
YOU DESERVE IT TOO
FOR WHAT YOU'VE BEEN THOUGH
SO OPEN YOUR HEART
SO HURRY AND START
JOIN ME ON MY PATH
AVOID THE WORLD'S WRATH
IT'S EASY TO DO
START BY LOVING YOU
AND THEN SPREAD THE LOVE
TO THE WORLD ABOVE
AT EIGHTY TWO YEARS
YOU ARE LOVING DEARS
WISHING LOVE TO ALL
FAST WITHOUT A STALL
SEE YOU IN TEN MORE
USE THE OPEN DOOR
LET ENERGY FLOW
AND ENJOY LIFE'S GLOW

EGO

EGO CONTROLS
YOU PLAY YOUR ROLES
YOU'RE FULL OF FEAR
INNER VOICE YOU HEAR
TELLS WHAT TO DO
MANAGES YOU
YOU CAN'T LET GO
YOU'RE IN THE SHOW
THEN YOU WAKE UP
PUT DOWN YOUR CUP
YOU SEE A LIGHT
IT'S A NEW FIGHT
WHICH IS YOUR SIDE
WHAT IS YOUR GUIDE
IS IT THE LOVE
LIGHT FROM ABOVE
YOU'RE NOW CONFUSED
GUIDANCE REFUSED
STRUGGLE ALONE
AND THEN YOU GROAN
WHAT CAN YOU DO
TO KNOW WHAT'S TRUE
YOU PLAY YOUR ROLES
EGO CONTROLS

EMPTY HEART

NO TIME FOR HEART
SO HOW CAN LOVE START
CHASING THE MONEY
LOSING YOUR HONEY
IT'S TIME TO WAKE UP
DOWN THE COFFEE CUP
CAN'T DO IT RIGHT NOW
MILK THE MONEY COW
JUST A LITTLE MORE
TO CLOSING THE DOOR

SO WHEN WILL I START
TO OPEN THE HEART
SURE I WANT TO CHANGE
BUT IT'S OUT OF RANGE
I NEED SOME MORE TIME
TO MAKE A NEW RHYME
IT'S SO HARD TO DO
TO FOLLOW CHANGE THROUGH
SO TRY AS I MAY
IN EVERY NEW WAY
I MUST SOON DECIDE
TO OPEN EYES WIDE
YES I NEED TO CHANGE
BUT IT'S OUT OF RANGE
MY HEART IS DYING
MY HONEY CRYING
NO TIME FOR HEART
SO HOW CAN LOVE START

EMPTY MIND

EMPTY MIND
PEACE YOU FIND
PLANT A SEED
NO MORE GREED
MONEY SLAVE
TO THE GRAVE
CHASING LOVE
GOD ABOVE
GETTING OLD
STORIES TOLD
YOUTH ANEW
IS FOR YOU
PEACE YOU FIND
EMPTY MIND

EVERYDAY

TRY AS I MAY
I FACE THE DAY
I DO ALL I COULD
I DO WHAT I SHOULD
ALL DAY LONG
WITH A SONG
IN MY HEART
FROM THE START
AS THE HOURS PASS
WALKING THROUGH THE GRASS
LOOKING AT THE SKY
OH HOW MUCH I TRY
TO FIND THE WAY
TO WORK AND PLAY
DO MY JOB SO WELL
ONLY TIME WILL TELL
WHERE I AM GOING
WITH MY HEART SHOWING
MY SOUL IS ALONE
MY VOICE MAKES A GROAN
AND THEN I THINK
WITHOUT A BLINK
TRY AS I MAY
I FACE THE DAY

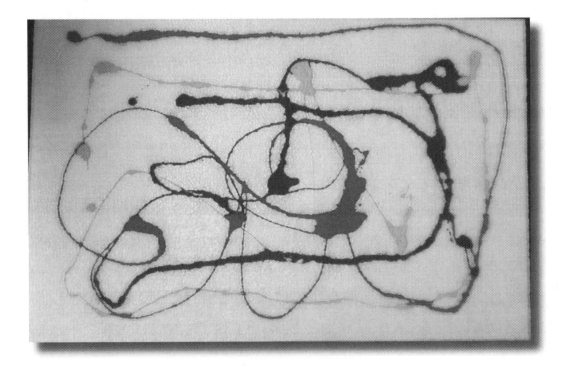

FAKE SUCCESS

YOUR FAKE SUCCESS
GIVES YOU DURESS
THEY TAUGHT YOU LIES
YOU THINK YOU'RE WISE
BUT STOP AND LOOK
AND CLOSE THE BOOK
AND LOOK AROUND
AND HEAR THE SOUND
IT'S NATURE'S VOICE
YOU HAVE A CHOICE
CLOSE THE CELL PHONE
YOU'RE NOT ALONE
COMPUTER TOO
OWNS PART OF YOU
SHUT THE TV
AND LEARN TO SEE
GET YOURSELF FREE
AND LEARN TO BE
YOUR OWN GOOD SELF
THE JUNGLE ELF
WHOSE LIFE IS REAL
DON'T LET THEM STEAL
YOUR HEART AND MIND
AND MAKE YOU BLIND
WITH FAKE SUCCESS
LIVING A MESS

FALSE IDEALS

FALSE IDEALS
TURNING THE WHEELS
THAT OWN YOUR MIND

AND MAKE YOU BLIND
THINGS THEY TAUGHT YOU
HOW THEY BOUGHT YOU
YOU HAD NO CHOICE
THEY STOLE YOUR VOICE
YOU DID NOT KNOW
FROM HEAD TO TOE
THEY FED YOU LIES
NOW YOU'RE NOT WISE
AND AS YOU THINK
QUICK AS A BLINK
YOUR MIND DOES SINK
YOUR BRAIN DOES SHRINK
IT CAN NOT GROW
YOU CAN NOT KNOW
LOCKED IN CEMENT
ENERGY SPENT
ON FALSE IDEALS
TURNING THE WHEELS

FEAR

LIVING IN FEAR
SO FAR SO NEAR
WHAT WILL YOU DO
THE BEST OF YOU
GO RUN AND HIDE
WHERE IS YOUR PRIDE
SO USE YOUR MIND
AND FIND LIKE KIND
AFTER THE TALK
DO THE RIGHT WALK
STAND UP BE BRAVE
GIVE UP THE SLAVE
WILL YOU DECIDE
GOD ON YOUR SIDE
SO FAR SO NEAR
LIVING IN FEAR

FEAR (2)

WHAT IS YOUR FEAR
KEEP YOUR MIND CLEAR
THEN YOU WILL SEE
THE WAY TO BE
AND WHEN YOU DO
FEAR WILL LEAVE YOU
YOU SEE THE LIGHT
THERE IS NO FIGHT
ALL BECOMES PEACE
YOUR FEARS WILL CEASE
HURRY AND START
AND DO YOUR PART
KEEP YOUR MIND CLEAR
THEN YOU LOSE FEAR

FEAR (3)

LET GO OF YOUR FEAR
THEN YOUR GOAL IS NEAR
MORE FORWARD EACH DAY
HEED NOT WHAT THEY SAY
ONLY YOU KNOW
THE WAY TO GO
STAY CLOSE TO YOUR HEART
IT TELLS WHERE TO START
LISTEN TO YOUR MIND
DIRECTION YOU'LL FIND
FEAR NOT TOMORROW
LIVE WITHOUT SORROW
PRACTICE ALL DAY LONG
AND NEVER SO WRONG
LET GO OF YOUR FEAR
THEN YOU GOAL IS HERE

FIGHT FOR PEACE

FIGHT FOR PEACE NOW
WAR MONEY COW
STOP THE MACHINE
ONLY DEATH IS SEEN
PEOPLE POWER
MAKE LOVE SHOWER
AND WAIT NO MORE
OPEN NEW DOOR
AND FIND NEW WAY
PEACE EVERY DAY
AND TAKE THE TIME
TO READ THIS RHYME
USE YOUR GOOD VOICE
IT IS YOUR CHOICE
THE TIME IS SHORT
LIFE WILL ABORT
SO STOP AND THINK
BEFORE YOU SINK
DO SOMETHING NOW
KILL THE WAR COW

FINDING YOUR WAY

FINDING YOUR WAY
EVERY NEW DAY
STOP FEEL YOUR HEART
THAT'S WHERE TO START
AND USE YOUR MIND
GOLD YOU WILL FIND
YOUR SPIRIT TOO
INSIDE OF YOU
SO ALL THE THREE
AND YOU WILL SEE
MIRACLES CLEAR
LOVING YOU DEAR
SO NOW YOU KNOW
THE WAY TO GO

EVERY NEW DAY
FINDING YOUR WAY

FIVE O'CLOCK

DID YOU EVER WANT TO STOP
THOUGH YOU DID NOT REACH THE TOP
YOU LOOKED AROUND
AND THERE YOU FOUND
NATURE'S BEAUTIFUL THINGS
SOARING ON EAGLE'S WINGS
YOU SAW THE TREES
THE COLORED LEAVES
THE DOGS AND CATS
THE RUNNING RATS
EVEN THE MICE
THEY LOOKED SO NICE
THE MOON, THE SUN, THE STARS
ALL THE PLANET AND MARS
VERY HIGH MOUNTAINS
ITALIAN FOUNTAINS
LOOKED AT THE CLOCK
YOU WERE SO SHOCKED
TWO MORE HOURS TO GO
YOU MUST MAKE A GOOD SHOW
GET YOUR WORK DONE
HOME TO HAVE FUN
IT WAS ALL A DREAM
AND SO IT DID SEEM
DID YOU EVER WANT TO STOP
THOUGH YOU DID NOT REACH THE TOP

FOLLOW THE RULES

FOLLOW THE RULES
AND PLAY THE FOOLS
DO WHAT YOU'RE TOLD
UNTIL YOU'RE OLD

KEEP YOUR BELIEFS
SOLD BY THE THIEVES
AND STAY ASLEEP
DON'T MAKE A PEEP
REPEAT WHAT TOLD
AND HIDE YOUR GOLD
HEAR YOUR MASTER
AND RUN FASTER
HE KNOWS THE WAY
SO STOP AND PRAY
DO WHAT YOU'RE TOLD
UNTIL YOU'RE OLD

FOOL

TECHNOLOGY
PSYCHOLOGY
THEY OWN YOUR MIND
THEY KEEP YOU BLIND
ARE YOU ASLEEP
DON'T MAKE A PEEP
SILENCE YOUR WAY
YOU PAY AND PAY
YOU BUY AND BUY
YOU NEVER SIGH
I WONDER WHY
YOU BUY THE LIE
BECAUSE YOU'RE STUCK
LIKE SITTING DUCK
YOUR MIND FROZEN
YOUR BRAIN DOZEN
NEVER YOU WAKE
THEY EAT YOUR CAKE
PSYCHOLOGY
TECHNOLOGY

FOOLS

WORLD OF FOOLS
WITH WRONG TOOLS
ZOMBIES SLEEP
DIE LIKE SHEEP
GREAT BRAND NAMES
CAUSE THE PAINS
CANNOT THINK
AND SO SINK
TIME HAS COME
MAYBE SOME
WILL AWAKE
ACTION TAKE
WORLD OF FOOLS
WITH NO TOOLS

FOUR SEASONS

FOUR SEASONS
GOOD REASONS
CHANGING ALL
SUMMER FALL
LIKE YOUR LIFE
AND YOUR WIFE
ALWAYS THERE
EVERYWHERE
SEEKING MORE
GOLDEN DOOR
OPEN THE HEART
THERE TO START
GOOD REASONS
FOUR SEASONS

FREEDOM

SEEK FREEDOM NOW
THEY'LL MILK YOUR COW
THEY OWN YOUR LAND
AND ALL THE SAND
THE OCEANS TOO
ALL PARTS OF YOU
AND AS YOU SLEEP
AND ACT LIKE SHEEP
FOLLOW THE RULES
AND LIVE LIKE FOOLS
YOUR THOUGHTLESS MIND
EYES SO BLIND
CAN YOU AWAKE
AND ACTION TAKE
AND USE YOUR BRAIN
AND RID THE PAIN
ARE YOU AFRAID
AND STAY THEIR MAID
SERVING THEIR NEEDS
DOING THEIR DEEDS
OH WHAT A SHAME
YOU ARE TO BLAME
YOU LIVE IN DARK
GO DISNEY PARK
AND PAY WITH SWEAT
WITH NO REGRET
BECAUSE YOU SLEEP
WILL BE DEAD SHEEP

FREEDOM

SET YOURSELF FREE
SO YOU CAN BE
PEACEFUL AND TRUE
THE BEST IN YOU
WITH OPEN HEART
AND A NEW START
AND WAIT NO MORE
WALK THROUGH THE DOOR
AND SEE THE LIGHT
SHINING SO BRIGHT
SO CLEAR YOUR MIND

THERE YOU WILL FIND
ALL YOU CAN BE
WHEN YOU ARE FREE

FREEDOM (2)

YOU ARE NOT FREE
YOU CANNOT SEE
YOU'RE IN YOUR BOX
WITH DOUBLE LOCKS
YOU DREAM OF CHOICE
YOU HAVE NO VOICE
YOUR ILLUSION
YOUR CONFUSION
TRY AS YOU MAY
YOU'RE THERE TO STAY
TRY TO ESCAPE
ALL THE RED TAPE
YOU PAY YOUR TAX
YOU BREAK YOUR BACKS
YOU SWEAT AND STRAIN
YOU'RE FULL OF PAIN
THERE IS NO GAIN
YOUR LIFE IN VAIN
SO YOU PRETEND
AND YOU DEFEND
FOLLOW THE RULES
LIKE ALL THE FOOLS
YOU THINK YOU'RE OUT
WITH A GREAT SHOUT
YOU CANNOT SEE
YOU ARE NOT FREE

FROM FEAR TO LOVE

FROM FEAR TO LOVE
TO SKY ABOVE
LET GO OF FEAR

THEN CAN SEE CLEAR
FOLLOW YOUR HEART
THE WAY TO START
COURAGE TO BE
THE WAY YOU SEE
YOUR LIFE UNFOLD
AND MELT LIKE GOLD
SHINING SO BRIGHT
NOTHING TO FIGHT
SO TAKE THE CHANCE
AND DO LIFE'S DANCE
TO SKY ABOVE
FROM FEAR TO LOVE

FUNNY MONEY

FUNNY
MONEY
HONEY
BUNNY
SMALL TOY
BIG JOY
FUN GAME
NO NAME
WARM HEART
GOOD START
THUNDER
WONDER
LET'S GO
SEE SHOW
FUNNY
MONEY

GET UP AND WALK

IT'S TIME TO WALK
AND STOP THE TALK
ENOUGH BEEN SAID
IT'S FILLED MY HEAD
COURAGE NEEDED
WARNINGS HEEDED
NEW FIELDS SEEDED
THIEVES LIARS TREATED
YEARS OF DISGRACE
ALL OUT OF PLACE
AND AS YOU SLEPT
ACTING INEPT
LOSING YOUR MONEY
THAT'S NOT FUNNY
SO STOP THE TALK
GET UP AND WALK

GIVE MONEY

GIVE MONEY NOW
AND KILL THE COW
SELL ALL THE MEAT
ON LOCAL STREET
WHAT A GREAT SHAME
WHO IS TO BLAME
ENJOY THE STEAK
EAT FISH IN LAKE
AND CHICKEN TOO
NOT GOOD FOR YOU
WHEN YOU KILL LIFE
YOU FEEL NO STRIFE
YOU HAVE BEEN TRAINED

YOU HAVE BEEN MAIMED
AND SKIN YOUR WEAR
PEOPLE THEN STARE
YOU WANT MONEY
IT'S SAD NOT FUNNY
ANIMALS DIE
DON'T YOU WONDER WHY
LOOK IN YOUR MIND
SEARCH FOR THE KIND
PART THAT IS THERE
LOOK EVERYWHERE
AND YOU WILL FIND
YOU CAN BE KIND
HAVE COMPASSION
IT'S NEW FASHION
DON'T KILL FOR FOOD
AND CHANGE YOUR MOOD
WAKE UP YOUR HEART
IT'S A NEW START

GLOBAL GAME

THE GLOBAL GAME
OH WHAT A SHAME
OH WHAT A PAIN
CRIMINALS REIGN
THEY OWN YOUR LIVES
THEY F... YOUR WIVES
DESTROY YOUR KIDS
WITH VACCINE BIDS
ROB STEAL YOUR GOLD
HAVE STRANGLE HOLD
THE USA
HAS GONE ASTRAY
ENGLAND BREXIT
MAKING EXIST
CHINESE ELDERS
THE WORLD WELDERS
AND RUSSIA TOO
TELLS WHAT TO DO

THE GREAT POPE TOO
TELLS WHAT TO DO
LET'S HAVE A WAR
FROM SHORE TO SHORE
THE DOLLAR SHRINKS
WITH YOUR QUICK BLINKS
YOU CANNOT HIDE
YOU'VE LOST YOUIR PRIDE
YOUR PRAYERS ALL FAIL
THEY OWN THE GRAIL
YOU WAIT AND SEE
FUTURE TO BE
THEY CREATE FEAR
YOUR LIFE'S NOT DEAR
SO GO AHEAD
AND BACK TO BED
BUT IF YOU THINK
AND CLEANSE THE STINK
THERE IS NO SHAME
JUST GLOBAL GAME

GOD GUIDE ME

GOD BE MY GUIDE
I'VE NOTHING TO HIDE
DON'T KNOW WHAT TO DO
SO I'M ASKING YOU
SHOULD I DO THIS OR THAT
BEFORE I GO TO BAT
I LOOK TO THE SKY
SO DON'T BE SHY
I SEE A WHITE BIRD
A GOOD SIGN I'VE HEARD
WHAT DOES IT MEAN
PLEASE GOD COME CLEAN
I HAVE TO KNOW
WHICH WAY TO GO
I NEED TO DECIDE
PLEASE GOD BE MY GUIDE

GOD IS WITH ME

GOD IS WITH ME
YES HE IS
I'M A TREE
I'M SHOW BIZ
WHATEVER I DO
I'M A SKY BLUE
I'M GREEN GRASS
THE BIG MASS
THE OCEAN THE SUN THE STARS
JUPITER PLUTO MARS
IT'S ALL THE SAME
PLAYING THE GAME
IN GOD'S NAME
GOD IS WITH ME ALL THE TIME
HELPING ME TO MAKE THIS RHYME

GOD SAID

GOD SAID LET THERE BE LIGHT
AND MAN BEGAN TO FIGHT
THERE WAS A LOT OF PAIN
BETWEEN ABLE AND CAIN
PULLED FROM ADAMS' RIB WAS EVE
SOON AFTER SHE DID CONCEIVE
MANY PEOPLE WERE BAD
THEN GOD THOUGHT: OH HOW SAD
HE TOLD NOAH WHAT TO DO
THE BAD PEOPLE WOULD BE THROUGH
NOAH SURE DID BELIEVE
KNOWING GOD WOULDN'T DECEIVE
THEN FORTY DAYS OF RAIN
HOWEVER ALL IN VAIN
MANKIND HAS NOT LEARNED YET
KILLING HE MUST FORGET
WILL GOD'S WRATH RETURN
AND MAKE THE WORLD BURN
WHAT SHOULD GOOD PEOPLE DO

THE FOLKS LIKE ME AN YOU
CAN WE CHANGE THE OTHERS
AND MAKE THEM GOOD BROTHERS
IF IT CAN BE DONE
WE'LL ALL HAVE SOME FUN
THE WORLD WILL BE HERE TO STAY
LIVING HAPPY EVERYDAY

GOD TAKE ME

GOD TAKE ME I'M YOURS
I'LL DO ALL THE CHORES
MY LIFE BELONGS TO YOU
NO MATTER WHAT I DO
HOWEVER I THINK
YES I'M ON THE BRINK
OF THOSE GREAT THINGS
ON EAGLE'S WINGS
FLYING HIGH
IN THE SKY
WITH ENDLESS LOVE
AND FAR ABOVE
AS I LOOK DOWN
MAN'S FACE HAS A FROWN
HE HAS GONE HIS OWN WAY
AND NOW HE HAS TO PAY
THE PRICE FOR HIS GREED
OVERGROWN WITH WEED
THAT HE TRIES TO KILL
BUT HE LACKS THE WILL
TO GIVE HIMSELF TO YOU
AND REMEMBER WHO
YOU REALLY ARE
EVER SO FAR
YET ALWAYS HERE
DISPELLING FEAR
GOD TAKE ME I'M YOURS
TO THE GOLDEN SHORES

GOD'S DAY

IT'S GOD'S DAY
TIME TO PRAY
SO START NOW
AND BOW
TO THE HEAVENS ABOVE
AND SHOW YOUR LOVE
TO EVERYTHING YOUR EYES CAN SEE
AND PLEASE DON'T FORGET ABOUT ME

GOD'S WORD

GOD'S WORD
MUST BE HEARD.
WHEN GOD TAKES THE LEAD
THE PEOPLE WILL HEED.
THE BIBLE SAYS THIS
THAT WE WILL NOT MISS.
THE LESSON IS ALMOST LEARNED
AND THE STONE IS BEING TURNED
JUST A LITTLE BIT MORE
TO REACH THE GOLDEN SHORE.
THEN WE WILL LIVE IN PEACE.
VIOLENCE AND WAR WILL CEASE.
THIS MUST BE HEARD
FOR IT'S GOD'S WORD.

GOD'S WORLD

GOD'S WORLD
UNFURLED
OPEN TO YOU
YES IT'S TRUE
IF YOU BELIEVE
YOU WILL CONCEIVE
ALL THAT IS THERE
YES, EVERYWHERE

SO START THE DAY
IN A NEW WAY
AND YOU WILL FIND
THAT GOD IS KIND
GOD WON'T TELL YOU WHAT TO DO
THAT'S ALWAYS UP TO YOU
IF YOUR THOUGHTS ARE GOOD
AND YOU DO WHAT YOU SHOULD
EVERYTHING YOU NEED
PROVIDED NO GREED
WILL SO BE YOURS
DOING YOUR CHORES
IN GOD'S WORLD
SO UNFURLED

GOOD HEART

IF YOU HAVE A GOOD HEART
YOU WILL KNOW WHERE TO START
PRACTICE EVERY DAY
THINGS WILL GO YOUR WAY
IF YOU FORGET
HAVE NO REGRET
TURN YOUR MIND AROUND
DO NOT MAKE A SOUND
LET ALL YOUR ACTIONS SHOW
YOU KNOW THE WAY TO GO
TREATING OTHERS WELL
ONLY TIME WILL TELL
KEEP YOURSELF AWARE
SURE TO DO YOUR SHARE
THEN YOU WILL SEE
YOU KNOW HOW TO BE
YOU KNOW WHAT TO DO
LOVE WILL COME TO YOU
YES A GOOD HEART
WILL HELP YOU START

GOOD MORNING

GOOD MORNING WORLD
OUT OF BED CURLED
OPEN MY EYES
SEE THE BLUE SKIES
OH IT'S SO NICE
TO HAVE A SLICE
OF A NEW DAY
LOVE COMES MY WAY
I SEE HER NEAR
MY DARLING DEAR
I TOUCH HER ARM
AND FEEL HER CHARM
GOOD MORNING WORLD
OUT OF BED CURLED

GOOD MORNING HEART

GOOD MORNING HEART
A DAY'S NEW START
OH WHAT A WAY
TO START THE DAY
LOVE ON MY MIND
HEART IS SO KIND
FEELING OF JOY
LIFE IS SUCH A TOY
AND FILLED WITH LOVE
SHINING SUN ABOVE
WITH SMILING FACE
ON HUMAN RACE
A DAY'S NEW START
GOOD MORNING HEART

GOOD OLD DAYS

THE GOOD OLD DAYS
THE GOOD OLD WAYS
USED TO BE FUN
NOW IT'S COP'S GUN
WE USED TO DANCE
AND HAVE ROMANCE
WE USED TO TALK
GO FOR A WALK
NOW IT'S CELL PHONES
AND KILLER DRONES
PLANES GO FASTER
WAR DISASTER
THINK BACK A WHILE
DAYS OF THE SMILE
BEAUTIFUL TUNES
BEWARE THE GOONS
AND AS YOU SIT
YOUR TEETH YOU GRIT
WHAT WILL COME NEXT
MESSAGE IN TEXT
IMPLANT YOUR CHIP
GO ON DRUG TRIP
LOOKING FOR PEACE
WARS NEVER CEASE
YOU SIT AND WAIT
SEARCH FOR YOU MATE
AS THE WORLD TURNS
AND NO ONE LEARNS
TO STOP AND SEE
HOW YOU COULD BE
THE GOOD OLD WAYS
THE GOOD OLD DAYS

GOODNIGHT

EVERY NIGHT WHEN I GO TO SLEEP
BEFORE I EVEN COUNT SHEEP
I LOOK UP AND PRAY
GOD GIVE ME ANOTHER DAY
I AM SO TIRED EVERY NIGHT
BECAUSE I DID EVERYTHING RIGHT
NOT EASY TO DO GOOD ALL DAY LONG
AND NEVER TO DO ANYTHING WRONG
I TRY TO MAKE EACH DAY A JOY
LIKE A CHILD PLAYING WITH A TOY
IT'S TIME TO LAY DOWN MY HEAD
PULL THE COVERS UP IN BED
AND AS I CLOSE MY EYES
AND IMAGINE BLUE SKIES
I SEE THE SHINNING STARS
AND THE RED PLANET MARS
AND I DRIFT OFF TO SLEEP
WITHOUT A SINGLE PEEP
AND ENDING THE DAY
IN A LOVELY WAY

GREAT BIG TREE

I WANT TO BE
A GREAT BIG TREE
SIT UNDER ME
AND YOU WILL SEE
ALL THAT I DO
SHELTERING YOU
A HOME TO BIRDS
SING LOVING WORDS
AND WHEN I'M DEAD
I MAKE YOUR BED
AND WHEN I BURN
GIVE HEAT IN TURN
SOME FRUIT I GIVE
SO YOU CAN LIVE

I CHANGE THE AIR
CLEAN EVERYWHERE
I NEVER DIE
NOW YOU KNOW WHY
I WANT TO BE
A GREAT BIG TREE

DO IT WITH PEP
WATCH THE BIG SHOW
START THE FOUNTAIN
LIFE WILL BE CLEAR
OH GREAT MOUNTAIN
LOVE WITHOUT FEAR

GREAT MOUNTAIN

OH GREAT MOUNTAIN
LOVE WITHOUT FEAR
START THE FOUNTAIN
LIFE WILL BE CLEAR
WATER FLOWING
EVERYTHING TRUE
SUN BEAMS GLOWING
BELONGS TO YOU
WARM BREATHE OF LIFE
YOU SEE THE SKY
AND WITHOUT STRIFE
AND WONDER WHY
I TREASURE THEE
THE OCEAN TOO
SO COME WITH ME
IS PART OF YOU
AND YOU WILL FIND
ALL LIVING THINGS
YOUR PEACE OF MIND
THE BIRD THAT SINGS
SO YOU WILL KNOW
THE YOUNG AND OLD
THE WAY TO GO
THE STORIES TOLD
SO TAKE THE STEP
SO HERE YOU GO

GREAT TREE

THANK YOU GREAT TREE
SHELTERING ME
YOU ARE SO STRONG
WITH ROOTS SO LONG
AND THERE I SIT
USING MY WIT
SEEKING TO FIND
ONE OF MY KIND
LOOK AS I MAY
SEARCHING ALL DAY
AND ALL I SEE
IS YOU AND ME
THANK YOU GREAT TREE
HOW I LOVE THEE

GREAT TREE (2)

OH GREAT TREE
TELL OF THEE
BRANCHES HIGH
IN THE SKY
LEAVES OF GREEN
BEAUTY SCENE
IN THE PARK
LIGHT AND DARK
ALWAYS THERE
STRONG AND FAIR
HOME TO BIRDS
SPEAK NO WORDS
TELL OF THEE
MY GREAT TREE

GUIDE ME

GOD GUIDE ME THROUGH MY LIFE
UNNECESSARY STRIFE
ALL OF US FACE EVERY DAY
AS WE EACH GO ON OUR WAY
SINCE THE BEGINNING OF TIME
THERE HAS ALWAYS BEEN SOME CRIME
SOME NEVER HAVE ENOUGH
AND MAKE THE HUMBLE TOUGH
WE LEARN TO SURVIVE
TO KEEP US ALIVE
AND DO THE THINGS WE MUST
BECAUSE WE LOST THE TRUST
AND RIGHTLY SO
OUR PATH WE GO
SEEKING OUR OWN ANSWERS
WATCHING ALL THE DANCERS
DOING WHAT THEY DO
TRYING TO FOOL YOU
INTO BELIEVING
THEY'RE NOT DECEIVING

SO BEWARE
GET YOUR SHARE
WITH GOD AS YOUR GUIDE
STANDING BY YOUR SIDE

GUIDE ME (2)

GOD, BE MY GUIDE.
I'VE NOTHING TO HIDE.
DON'T KNOW WHAT TO DO
SO I'AM ASKING YOU.
SHOULD I DO THIS OR THAT
BEFORE I GO TO BAT?
I LOOK TO THE SKY
SO DON'T BE SHY.
I SEE A WHITE BIRD
A GOOD SIGN I'VE HEARD
WHAT DOES IT MEAN?
PLEASE, GOD, COME CLEAN.
I HAVE TO KNOW
WHICH WAY TO GO.
I NEED TO DECIDE.
PLEASE, GOD, BE MY GUIDE.

H

HARD DRIVE

YOU'RE IN HARD DRIVE
SO YOU SURVIVE
TRAINED TO OBEY
EVERY NEW DAY
PROGRAM IS FIXED
YOU LIFE IS MIXED
SHOWER EAT SHAVE
COMPANY SLAVE
GET IN AT EIGHT
THAT IS YOUR FATE
YOU START TO THINK
AND YOUR EYES BLINK
NO WAY TO LIVE
YOU GIVE AND GIVE
YOU NEED TO CHANGE
YOUR LIFE REARRANGE
YOU THINK AND THINK
QUICK AS A WINK
WHAT CAN YOU DO
YOU FEEL SO BLUE
BUT YOU HAVE HOPE
A HARD DRIVE DOPE
IT'S NOT FOR ME
NOW THAT I SEE
ANOTHER WAY
TO LIVE THE DAY
I WILL SURVIVE
WITHOUT HARD DRIVE

HEALING LIGHT

OH HEALING LIGHT
PLEASE END THE FIGHT
STOP ALL THE WARS
OPEN ALL THE DOORS
FOCUS ON THE SOIL
NOT STEALING OIL
PUT LIGHT IN US ALL
SO WE DON'T FALL
OPEN THE BRAINS
TAKE OUT THE PAINS
HELP THE BLIND SEE
RIGHT WAY TO BE
SO EARTH CAN FIND
THE PEACE OF MIND
INFUSED WITH LIGHT
ALL DAY AND NIGHT

HEALTH

HEALTH FOR ALL
NONE WILL FALL
STAND UP TALL
BREAK YOUR WALL
HABITS DOWN
TOES TO CROWN
LET THINGS GO
THEN YOU KNOW
HEAL YOUR LIFE
NO MORE STRIFE
ALL IS GOOD
AS IT SHOULD
HEALTH FOR ALL
NONE WILL FALL

HEAR THE HEART'S VOICE

HEAR THE HEART'S VOICE
IT IS YOUR CHOICE
FEEL THE HEART'S LOVE
BELOW ABOVE
ON ALL THE SIDES
LOVE ALWAYS RIDES
BONDS YOU WITH ALL
SO HEAR LOVE'S CALL
SO SOFT AND WARM
TOUCHES EVERY FORM
ALL WITHOUT WORDS
LIKE SONGS OF BIRDS
SO MAKE THE CHOICE
HEAR THE HEART'S VOICE

HEART

POUR OUT YOUR HEART
THAT'S WHERE TO START
LET GO OF FEAR
I LOVE YOU DEAR
LET YOUR LOVE SHINE
SWEET GLASS OF WINE
FULL OF YOUR LOVE
LIKE PURE WHITE DOVE
ENCIRCLE THE SKY
WONDER NOT WHY
WARM STREAMS OF JOY
LOVE IS HEART'S TOY
REMEMBER THIS
LOVE IS HEART'S BLISS
THAT'S WHERE TO START
POUR OUT YOUR HEART

HEART (2)

GREAT HEART DOES SPEAK
LOVE CHEEK TO CHEEK
AND THERE WE STAND
IN NO MAN'S LAND
LOVE WE NOW FEEL
WITH HEART'S GOOD SEAL
MOMENT OF JOY
A GIRL A BOY
THERE TOGETHER
JUST ONE FEATHER
CHEEK TO CHEEK LOVE
SUN MOON SKY ABOVE

HEART (3)

FROZEN HEART
BROKE APART
PIECES FALL
OVER ALL
TOUCH THE GROUND
WITHOUT SOUND
BEGIN GROWING
LIFE'S SHOWING
PIECES FIND
SOMEONE KIND
LOVING EYES
NO MORE CRIES
WARM HEART
NOT APART

HEART LIGHT

WHEN YOUR HEART LIGHT
CAN SHINE SO BRIGHT
ALL DAY AND NIGHT
YOU LOOSE THE FIGHT

THAT'S IN YOUR MIND
AND BECOME KIND
AND THERE YOU FIND
HOW TO UNWIND
IT BECOMES CLEAR
YOU LOOSE ALL FEAR
WHEN YOUR HEART LIGHT
WILL SHINE SO BRIGHT

WITH NATURE'S MIND
AND YOU WILL FIND
YOU ARE ALL PART
A NEW WORLD START
IT'S YOUR LIFE'S GAIN
BE FREE OF PAIN

HEART RISING

YOU HAVE NO CHOICE
YOU HAVE NO VOICE
YOUR MIND CONTROLLED
THEIR PLAN UNFOLD
YOUR HEART DESTROYED
YOUR LOVE MADE VOID
UNLESS YOU RISE
AND BECOME WISE
NOW YOU MUST START
TO TRUST YOUR HEART
RENEW YOUR LIFE
END THE WORLD'S STRIFE
HEART REVOLUTION
OUR EVOLUTION

HEART REVOLUTION

HEART REVOLUTION
LOVE IS SOLUTION
YOU MUST LOOK INSIDE
LET LOVE BE YOUR GUIDE
LEARN HOW TO DO IT
SLOWLY BIT BY BIT
TAKE ALL TIME YOU NEED
LEARN TO PLANT THE SEED
THE SEED OF YOUR LOVE
FED BY RAIN ABOVE
FED BY EARTH BELOW
LET YOUR GOOD HEART SHOW
LET IN SUNSHINE TOO
SEE THE BEST IN YOU
IT'S ALWAYS BEEN THERE
BEHIND THE COLD STARE
LOVE IS SOLUTION
NEW REVOLUTION

HEART'S BRAIN

HEAR YOUR HEART'S BRAIN
IT'S YOUR LIFE'S GAIN
THE HEART CAN FEEL
YES IT IS REAL
YOUR HEART CAN THINK
IT'S YOUR LIFE'S LINK
CONNECT TO YOUR BRAIN
AND LEARN TO TRAIN
THE CONNECTION
DEEP REFLECTION

HEART SOUL
AND SPIRIT

HEART SOUL AND SPIRIT
LISTEN AND HEAR IT
STAY STILL FOR A WHILE
THEN STOP AND SMILE
THEN YOUR HEART GETS WARM
FEELINGS START TO FORM
NOW MUCH MORE ALIVE

NEW LIFE STARTS TO THRIVE
JOY FILLS ALL THE SPACE
THEN NEW HUMAN RACE
LISTEN AND HEAR IT
HEART SOUL AND SPIRIT

HEART VIBRATION

HEART VIBRATION
OF THE NATION
LOVE FILLS ALL
SHORT AND TALL
LOOK AROUND
HEAR THE SOUND
LOVING BEAT
GIVES THE HEAT
JOIN THE TUNE
DO IT SOON
FEEL THE JOY
PLAY LOVES TOY
HEART VIBRATION
OF THE NATION

HELLO GOODBYE

HELLO GOODBYE
I WONDER WHY
YOUR SMILING FACE
THE HUMAN RACE
PLEASE TELL ME HOW
TO NATURE BOW
AND GIVE UP WAR
OPEN LOVE'S DOOR
FOR ALL TO SEE
THE WAY TO BE
THE TIME IS HERE

LET GO OF FEAR
I WONDER WHY
HELLO GOODBYE

HELLO MY FRIEND

HELLO MY FRIEND
LET'S START NOT END
SO DO YOU KNOW
LIFE IS A SHOW
START'S WHEN YOU'RE BORN
FROM MOTHER TORN
THEN OUT YOU COME
MILK YOU HAVE SOME
THEN YOU ARE CHILD
START TO GO WILD
AND AS YOU GROW
THE TEACHERS SHOW
THEY FEED YOU LIES
YOU CAN'T BE WISE
THE TV TOO
STARTS TO OWN YOU
THEN THE CELL PHONE
MAKES YOU A DRONE
SOON YOU GROW OLD
YOU LOOK FOR GOLD
AND WHAT YOU FIND
YOU'RE A BIT BLIND
BY THEN IT'S LATE
YOU'RE AT THE GATE
GOODBYE MY FRIEND
YOU'RE AT THE END

HELP ME

WORLD CRIES HELP ME
SO CAN'T YOU SEE
WE ARE IN NEED

BELIEVE NEW CREED
COOPERATE
WOULD BE SO GREAT
WORK TOGETHER
BIRDS OF FEATHER
WE'RE ALL THE SAME
PLEASE STOP THE BLAME
WE ACT SO LAME
IT'S SUCH A SHAME
EACH WANT SOME MORE
TILL DEATH'S DOOR
THE THOUGHTLESS MIND
CAN NEVER FIND
THE PEACE YOU SEEK
TO BECOME MEEK
TO BECOME STRONG
TO LIVE SO LONG
SO WHERE TO LOOK
YOU'VE TRIED THE BOOK
THEN YOU AWAKE
NEW LOOK YOU TAKE
MAYBE YOU SEE
IF YOU HELP ME

HERE I GO AGAIN

SEVENTY YEARS OLD
I'VE SEEN LIFE UNFOLD
FEEL YOUNG AT HEART
WANT A NEW START
LOOKING FOR LOVE
HELP ME FROM ABOVE
SO THAT I FIND
SOME PEACE OF MIND
THE LOVE OF MY LIFE
WILL BECOME MY WIFE
HEART WILL BE FULFILLED
AND MY BODY THRILLED
SOME STORY TO TELL

AND ALL WILL BE WELL
HERE I GO AGAIN
NEVER KNOWING WHEN

HOME

WHERE IS HOME
MUCH I ROAM
ALL THE SAME
LIFE'S A GAME
PLAY IT WELL
BUY AND SELL
GET MONEY
FOR YOUR HONEY
GIVE A KISS
NEVER MISS
TOUCH HER HEART
LOVE WILL START
MUCH I ROAM
I AM HOME

HOPE

SOME STILL HAVE HOPES
WE'RE NOT ALL DOPES
THE GREAT SPIRIT
NOW CAN HEAR IT
VOICES ARISE
FROM ALL THE WISE
THEY WILL ARREST
THOSE THEY DETEST
AND SOLDIERS TOO
KNOW WHAT TO DO
YES TIME FOR CHANGE
IT'S IN THE RANGE
ENERGY STRONG
AGAINST THE WRONG
FROM THOSE WHO SEE

BEGINS WITH THEE
SO LIFT YOUR HEAD
MIND OUT OF BED
AND DO YOUR PART
LIGHT UP YOUR HEART
WE'RE ALL NOT DOPES
RAISE UP YOUR HOPES

HOPE (2)

GOD TELL ME WHAT TO DO
I WANT TO FOLLOW YOU
I WANT TO FILL MY HEART
TO MAKE A BRIGHT NEW START
I'LL LEAVE ALL MY OLD WAYS
TO START LIVING NEW DAYS

HOPE (3)

I'M ON MY WAY
FOR A NEW DAY
THE PAST IS BEHIND
I KNOW I WILL FIND
EVERYTHING I NEED
ROSES NOT A WEED
AS I LOOK AHEAD
NOT A TEAR I'LL SHED
ALL IS FRESH AND NEW
I'LL EVEN FIND YOU
MY OUTLOOK IS FINE
THE BRIGHT SUN WILL SHINE
I'VE LEARNED WHAT TO DO
WITH THE OLD I'M THROUGH
I HAVE SO MUCH HOPE
IT'S A GOLDEN ROPE
TO PULL ALONG
WITH NATURE'S SONG
YES HOPE ABOVE ALL

LIFT ME FROM A MY FALL
SO HERE I COME
READY FOR SOME
YES I'M ON MY WAY
FOR A BRIGHT NEW DAY

HOPE AND ILLUSION

YOUR BIG HOPE IS YOUR ILLUSION
REALITY YOUR INTRUSION
SO A LITTLE OF EACH
SO GOOD TO LEARN AND TEACH
ANY THEN YOU WILL KNOW
WHICH WAY TO GO
FOR FLYING TOO HIGH
INTO THE BLUE SKY
WILL TAKE LONG TO RETURN
TO THE EARTH THAT YOU YEARN
YET KEEP YOUR HEAD UP HIGH
LIVE THE TRUTH NOT A LIE
AND WHEN TRUTH IS YOUR GUIDE
DON'T EVER NEED TO HIDE
FOR ONLY THERE YOU WILL FIND
SUCH A SIMPLE PEACE OF MIND
SAY GOODBYE TO ILLUSION
THAT WILL BE YOUR CONCLUSION

HOW DO YOU KNOW

HOW DO YOU KNOW
THE WAY TO GO
WHO IS YOUR GUIDE
THERE AT YOUR SIDE
HOW DO YOU THINK
THOUGHTS RISE OR SINK
EMOTIONS RULE
ONLY THE FOOL
SO LIFT YOU MIND

LEARN TO BE KIND
CONFUSION STRONG
AND LASTS SO LONG
THIS IS YOUR CHANCE
LEARN A NEW DANCE
THEN YOU WILL KNOW
THE WAY TO GO

MASTER'S TOOL
USELESS LIFE
ENDLESS STRIFE
A CLOSED MIND
NEVER FIND
THEN YOU DIE
DON'T KNOW WHY
BORN A SLAVE
DIG YOUR GRAVE

HUMANITY

LET THERE BE LIGHT
SO STOP THE FIGHT
IT IS NOT RIGHT
START A NEW SIGHT
AND THERE YOU SEE
THE WAY TO BE
IT IS ALL CLEAR
WHEN YOU LOSE FEAR
SO START RIGHT NOW
TO NATURE BOW
THEN SPREAD THE WORD
THE WORLD HAS HEARD
NEW WAY TO LIVE
LEARN HOW TO GIVE
SO STOP THE FIGHT
LET THERE BE LIGHT

HUMANITY (2)

BORN A SLAVE
STUPID KNAVE
SOUND ASLEEP
ZOMBIE SHEEP
NEVER WAKE
POWER TAKE
HAVE NO VOICE
HAVE NO CHOICE
DUMB DOWN FOOL

HURRY HURRY

HURRY HURRY
LOST MY WORRY
I MOVE SO FAST
A SPELL WAS CAST
AND ALL I SAW
AN OPEN DOOR
I WALKED RIGHT THROUGH
A WORLD SO NEW
OF LOVE AND PEACE
ALL WARS DID CEASE
COULD NOT BELIEVE
NO MORE DECEIVED
THEY TOLD THE TRUTH
THE LOVING YOUTH
THEY FREED THEIR MINDS
TOOK OFF THEIR BLINDS
LISTENED TO BIRDS
SAW HORSE HERDS
LIKE THE OLD DAYS
THE GOOD OLD WAYS
SO I WILL STOP
MY BRAIN WILL POP
I WILL HURRY
LOOSE MY WORRY

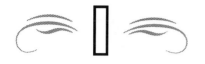

AND SO DID I
I DO NOT CRY
YES NOW AM I

I AM

I AM THE RAIN
I HAVE NO PAIN
I AM THE WIND
I AM THE EARTH
I AM THE SKY
I AM THE STARS
I AM THE CLOUDS
I AM THE TREES
I AM THE BEES
I AM THE ANTS
I AM FLOWERS
I AM THE FRUIT
I AM OCEANS
I AM THE LAKES
I AM THE HORSE
I AM THE DOG
I AM THE CAT
I AM THE RAT
I AM RIVERS
I AM PEOPLE
I AM THE STONES
AM EVERYTHING
THE BIRDS THAT SING
SO NOW YOU KNOW
ALL IS THE SHOW
SIT BACK ENJOY
THE PLANET'S TOY
FOR YOU ARE PART
OF THE NEW START
YOU ARE AWAKE
FOR GOODNESS SAKE
YOU ARE AWARE
LOST YOUR BLANK STARE

I AM A TREE

I AM A TREE
AND CAN'T YOU SEE
A HAVE A TRUNK
I DON'T EAT JUNK
I LOVE THE SUN
I HAVE NO GUN
BRANCHES ARE HIGH
REACHING FOR SKY
MY LEAVES ARE GREEN
NATURES GREAT SCENE
MY ROOTS ARE STRONG
AND VERY LONG
I STAND IN PEACE
MY LOVE WON'T CEASE
I CLEAN THE AIR
AND I PLAY FAIR
I PROTECT BIRDS
SEE MOVING HERDS
PLEASE RESPECT ME
I AM A TREE

I AM A TREE (2)

LIKE TO BE A TREE
THEN WHAT WOULD YOU SEE
EVERYTHING GOES BY
NOT EVEN A SIGH
BECAUSE ALL YOU KNOW
IS WATCHING THE SHOW
OF WEATHER AND LIFE
YOU HAVE NO MORE STRIFE
ALL YOU NEED IS SUN

WATER AND SOME FUN
AND THERE YOU STAND
YOU ARE SO GRAND
YOUR ROOTS ARE SO DEEP
NOT EVENT A PEEP
RAIN AND SNOW
MAKE YOU GROW
NO PLACE TO GO
SURELY YOU KNOW
IT'S GOOD TO BE
A GREAT BIG TREE

WHERE YOUR LOVE WILL GO
IF IT COMES MY WAY
I'LL HAVE A BRIGHT DAY
DON'T KNOW WHAT TO SAY
SO I'LL START TO PRAY
GOD WILL HEAR ME NOW
AS MY HEAD WILL BOW
RELEASING MY TEARS
GOODBYE TO MY FEARS
I CRY SO MUCH
I WANT YOUR TOUCH

I AM LIGHT

I AM LIGHT
I DON'T FIGHT
THINK THE SAME
LEAVE THE GAME
LEARN NEW WAYS
CHANGE YOUR DAYS
FIND YOUR PEACE
PAIN WILL CEASE
THEN YOU KNOW
IT WILL SHOW
TO YOUR FRIEND
MESSAGE SEND
I DON'T FIGHT
I AM LIGHT

I CRY SO MUCH

I CRY SO MUCH
I WANT YOUR TOUCH
TEARS SO MANY
NOT WORTH A PENNY
CAUSE YOU'RE NOT HERE
MY DARLING DEAR
PERHAPS YOU DON'T KNOW

I DON'T WANT TO LOSE YOUR LOVE

I DON'T WANT TO LOSE YOUR LOVE
MADE IN THE HEAVEN ABOVE
IF I DIDN'T TREAT YOU RIGHT
GIVE ME ANOTHER NIGHT
TO SHOW MY LOVE FOR YOU
BECAUSE IT'S REALLY TRUE
I'VE HAD MANY CHANCES
FOR OTHER ROMANCES
NONE SEEM TO BE RIGHT
THEY MAKE ME UPTIGHT
AFTER ALL THESE YEARS
AND SO MANY TEARS
TRIED AS I DID
COULDN'T GET RID
OF THOSE WAYS OF MINE
YOU SO VERY FINE
PLEASE TRY AGAIN
AND TELL ME WHEN
DON'T WANT TO LOSE YOUR LOVE
MADE IN HEAVEN ABOVE

I LOVE YOU

MOUNTAIN GREEN
WHAT A SCENE
SKY SO BLUE
I LOVE YOU
TREES SO TALL
NEVER FALL
FLOWERS TOO
I LOVE YOU
RIVERS COLD
VERY OLD
OCEANS TOO
I LOVE YOU
NATURE TRUE
I LOVE YOU

IF WE HAD A HEART

IF CORPORATIONS HAD A HEART
IF CEO'S HAD A HEART
IF WORLD LEADERS HAD A HEART
IF MONEY HAD A HEART
IF YOU HAD A HEART
IF THE WORLD HAD A HEART
IF WE COOPERATED
IF WE RESPECTED NATURE
IF WE STOPPED MAKING WEAPONS
IF WE PLANTED MORE FOOD
IF WE CLEANED THE AIR
IF WE CLEANED THE WATER
IF WE CLEANED THE EARTH
IF WE CLEANED OUR MINDS
IF WE RESPECTED EACH OTHER
IF WE LOVED EACH OTHER
IF WE PRACTICED ALL THE ABOVE
IF WE LIVED FROM OUR HEARTS
WHAT A WORLD IT WOULD BE!

ILLUSION

LIFE'S ILLUSION
YOUR CONFUSION
YOU CHASE YOUR DREAM
THEN IF DOES SEEM
YOU'VE REACHED YOUR GOAL
YOU'VE PAID THE TOLL
THEN YOU AWAKE
AND TRY TO TAKE
ANOTHER LOOK
AT A NEW BOOK
AND THERE YOU FIND
ANOTHER KIND
A NEW IDEA
IT BECOMES CLEAR
YOU THINK YOU KNOW
NEW WAY TO GO
AGAIN YOU TRY
NEW KIND OF SIGH
ONLY TO FIND
YOU ARE BLIND
NEW CONFUSION
LIFE'S ILLUSION

ILLUSIONS

ILLUSIONS
INTRUSIONS
CONFUSIONS
MUCH WORRIES
GREAT HURRIES
MANY FEARS
CRYING TEARS
SUCH BIG DOUBTS
MANY SHOUTS
FUTURE THOUGHTS
LIFE ABORTS
CLUTTERED MIND

PEACE CAN'T FIND
WANTING MORE
BUY THE STORE
STOP AND THINK
QUICK AS WINK
CHANGE YOUR LIFE
END THE STRIFE
BE LIKE ME
BE A TREE

IN LOVE'S ARMS

IN LOVE'S ARMS
FEEL YOUR CHARMS
SEE YOUR EYES
FEEL YOUR THIGHS
ARE NO LIES
HEAR YOUR SIGHS
SO WE ARE
VERY FAR
IN THE HEART
FROM THE START
JUST PURE LOVE
RAINS ABOVE
FEEL YOUR CHARMS
IN LOVE'S ARMS

INNER PEACE

FIND INNER PEACE
TROUBLE WILL CEASE
WHERE DO YOU LOOK
NOT IN A BOOK
YOURSELF TO BE
THEN YOU CAN SEE
YOU LOOK INSIDE
YOU DO NOT HIDE
YOU GO DEEPER

YOUR OWN KEEPER
SILENT YOU ARE
FROM WORLD SO FAR
LET GO LET GO
FAR FROM THE SHOW
MAINTAIN YOUR STANCE
NOT IN LIFE'S DANCE
NOW CLOSE YOUR EYES
AND DROP LIFE'S SIGHS
DO IT RIGHT NOW
TO YOURSELF BOW
YOU DRIFT AWAY
AND THERE YOU STAY
TROUBLE WILL CEASE
IN INNER PEACE

IN THE MIDDLE

DO YOU BEGIN
WITH A BIG GRIN
IDEAS ARE GOOD
THE WAY THEY SHOULD
THEN WHAT IS NEXT
ARE YOU PERPLEXED
WHAT SHALL YOU DO
IT'S UP TO YOU
TRY THIS AND THAT
YOU GO TO BAT
OH WHAT WILL WORK
YOU'RE NOT A JERK
YOU THINK AND THINK
AND THEN YOU SINK
YOU LOSE PASSION
YOUR TIME YOU RATION
YOU ARE THEN STUCK
YOU PASS THE BUCK
WITH LITTLE CHOICE
YOU LOSE YOU VOICE
BECAUSE YOU FIND
NO PEACE OF MIND

INCH BY INCH

INCH BY INCH
IT'S A CINCH
WIN THE GAME
IT'S NO SHAME
ARE NO RULES
ONLY FOOLS
FOLLOW NORMS
DROWN IN STORMS
LEARN THE WAY
HOW TO STAY
EACH NEW DAY
THAT'S THE PLAY
IT'S A CINCH
INCH BY INCH

INNER PEACE

INNER PEACE
CELL PHONE CEASE
BE ALONE
SHUT THE PHONE
INTERNET
NO REGRET
SELLING ALL
PLEASE DON'T FALL
WHAT'S UNTRUE
BESTING YOU
GET AWAKE
FOR YOUR SAKE
CELL PHONE CEASE
INNER PEACE

INSANE WORLD

EVERYDAY I FEEL THE PAIN
HOW THE WORLD HAS GONE INSANE
PEOPLE CANNOT LIVE IN PEACE
WHEN WILL ALL THIS HORROR CEASE
LOOKING BACK IN HISTORY
WE KNOW IT'S NO MYSTERY
EVEN ABLE AND CAIN
UNABLE TO SUSTAIN
HARMONY AND PEACE
AND LOVE THEN DID CEASE
ANGER TAKES ITS TOLL
AND DRAINS OUT ONE'S SOUL
BUT IF YOU STAY ALERT
YOU DON'T NEED TO BE HURT
SO KEEP YOUR MIND AWARE
DO EVERYTHING THAT'S FAIR
PUT ASIDE YOUR GREED
AND PLANT THE GOOD SEED
IN YOUR CHILDREN'S MIND
FOR THERE YOU WILL FIND
THE POTENTIAL FOR LOVE
THE BEAUTIFUL WHITE DOVE
THAT SINGS THE SWEET SONG
AND FLIES ALL DAY LONG
AND RELIEVES THE PAIN
IN THIS WORLD INSANE

INTERNET

INTERNET SLAVE
UNTIL YOUR GRAVE
I AM THERE TOO
AM JUST LIKE YOU
CAN WE ESCAPE
MIND CONTROL RAPE
THE CELL PHONE TOO
ALSO OWNS YOU
WHERE CAN WE TURN
MIND CONTROL BURN
WHAT WILL COME NEXT
ARE YOU PERPLEXED
ROBOTS ARE HERE

AND MAKE YOU FEAR
YOU ARE REPLACED
SO MAKE YOUR HASTE
BEFORE YOU'RE DONE
AND SEARCH FOR FUN
BEFORE YOUR GRAVE
INTERNET SLAVE

IT IS ALL IN YOU

IT IS ALL IN YOU
WHEN YOU THINK IT THROUGH
ALL YOU NEED TO KNOW
EVERYWHERE YOU GO
COUNT ON YOUR SKILLS
WHEN YOU HAVE ILLS
NOT DOCTOR'S PILLS
TO END YOUR CHILLS
IF YOU STOP AND THINK AWHILE
YOU WILL BEGIN TO SMILE
YOU HAVE ALL THE ANSWERS INSIDE
WHEN YOU LEARN OPEN AND NOT HIDE
LOOK INSIDE YOURSELF
YOU'LL FIND A GOOD ELF
WHO'S THERE TO HELP YOU WITH ALL YOU DO
GOOD ELF WILL ALWAYS SEE YOU THROUGH
WHATEVER CIRCUMSTANCE YOU'RE IN
YOU WILL CERTAINLY ALWAYS WIN
BECAUSE IT IS ALL IN YOU
WHEN YOU THINK IT THROUGH

IT'S ALL ABOUT LOVE

IT'S ALL ABOUT LOVE
FROM THE GOD ABOVE
WE NEED SOME EVERYDAY
TO FEEL GOOD ON THE WAY

WHEREVER WE GO
IT WILL ALWAYS SHOW
HOW WE TREAT EACH OTHER
LIKE A FRIEND AND BROTHER
WITH LOVE IN THE HEART
WITH A BRAIN THAT'S SMART
YOU CAN DO ANYTHING
FLYING ON EAGLE'S WING
TO REACH YOUR GOAL
BECOMING WHOLE
JUST LIKE WHEN YOU WERE BORN
AND FROM YOUR MOTHER TORN
AND NOW THAT YOU ARE FREE
YOU ARE ABLE TO SEE
IT'S ALL ABOUT LOVE
YOU NEED SO MUCH OF

IT'S COMING NOW

IT'S COMING NOW
I'LL TELL YOU HOW
GOOD THINGS IN STORE
RIGHT AT YOUR DOOR
YOU'LL SEE THEM SOON
THEY'LL MAKE YOU SWOON
HAPPY YOU'LL BE
YOUR EYES WILL SEE
UP COME THE SPROUTS
YOU'LL HERE THE SHOUTS
RING THROUGH THE WORLD
BANNER UNFURLED
SO BREATHE REAL DEEP
IN PEACE YOU'LL SLEEP
I'LL TELL YOU HOW
IT'S COMING NOW

IT'S UP TO YOU

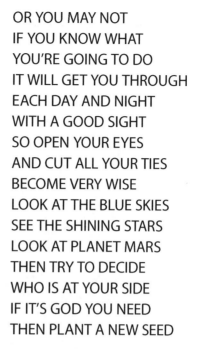

WHAT YOU CAN DO
IS UP TO YOU
WANT TO LIVE LONG
SING NATURE'S SONG
THEN YOU WILL ACHIEVE
NO MORE NEED TO GRIEVE
THE MORE YOU WILL DO
THE BETTER FOR YOU
IF YOU START TODAY
YOU WILL MAKE YOUR WAY
YOUR CHILDREN YOU WILL SAVE
NO LONGER BE A SLAVE
TO FALSE INFORMATION
MISLEADING THE NATION
WAKE UP YOUR MIND
TRUTH YOU WILL FIND
BECOME MORE AWARE
YOU ARE GETTING THERE
LEARNING PREVENTION
FREEING YOUR TENSION
LIFTING YOUR SPIRIT
LISTEN AND HEAR IT
DO ALL YOU CAN
MAKE A GOOD PLAN
WHAT YOU CAN DO
IS UP TO YOU

OR YOU MAY NOT
IF YOU KNOW WHAT
YOU'RE GOING TO DO
IT WILL GET YOU THROUGH
EACH DAY AND NIGHT
WITH A GOOD SIGHT
SO OPEN YOUR EYES
AND CUT ALL YOUR TIES
BECOME VERY WISE
LOOK AT THE BLUE SKIES
SEE THE SHINING STARS
LOOK AT PLANET MARS
THEN TRY TO DECIDE
WHO IS AT YOUR SIDE
IF IT'S GOD YOU NEED
THEN PLANT A NEW SEED

IT'S UP TO YOU (2)

IF IT'S GOD YOU NEED
THEN PLANT A GOOD SEED
REMOVE THE WEED
AND YOU'LL BE FREED
TO LIVE LIFE IN PEACE
YOUR TROUBLES WILL CEASE
IF YOU SO BELIEVE
THEN YOU WILL RECEIVE

J

JOY OR PAIN

JOY OR PAIN
NOT IN VAIN
SO IS LIFE
PEACE OR STRIFE
KEEP YOUR CALM
READ A PSALM
DARK OR LIGHT
LOVE OR FIGHT
MAKE YOUR CHOICE
USE YOUR VOICE
CLEARLY SEE
ALL YOU BE
JOY OR PAIN
NOT IN VAIN

JUDGMENT

THE PAIN OF MY LIFE INCREASES EVERYDAY
WHEN I HAVE LOVE IN MY HEART TO GIVE
I ALWAYS DO THE WRONG THING IN
EVERY WAY
I FEEL SO SAD SOMETIMES I DON'T WANT
TO LIVE
I'M TOLD TIME AND AGAIN I'M NO GOOD
I'M NEVER ABLE TO DO WHAT I SHOULD
I FEEL SO MISUNDERSTOOD
IT'S LIKE MY BRAIN IS MADE OF WOOD
I'M NEVER GIVEN THE CHANCE TO TALK AND
EXPLAIN
IT DOESN'T MATTER THAT I FEEL SO MUCH
PAIN
PLEASE FORGIVE MY MISUNDERSTOOD
DEEDS
O PLEASE NOURISH MY HEART WITH THE
LOVE IT NEEDS

LOVE IS YOUR GAME
YOU WILL NOT MISS
WITH A BIG KISS

KILLING FOR PEACE

KILLING FOR PEACE
WHEN WILL IT CEASE
HOW GREAT THE PAIN
CAUSED BY INSANE
CORPORATIONS
RUN THE NATIONS
WHAT IS THE GOAL
WHAT IS OUR ROLE
THINK HARD THINK CLEAR
YOUR LIFE MY DEAR
ITS ON THE LINE
AND SO IS MINE
SO WHAT TO DO
ITS UP TO YOU
WHEN WILL IT CEASE
KILLING FOR PEACE

KNOW IT ALL

YOUR MIND IS SMALL
THINK KNOW IT ALL
YOU SPEAK SO STRONG
BUT DON'T LAST LONG
YOU ACT SO YANG
LIKE TIGER'S FANG
YOUR STRENGTH YOU SHOW
LIKE A BENT BOW
CONQUER YOUR FRIENDS
TO NO GOOD ENDS
YOU FLY SO HIGH
YOU DON'T KNOW WHY
YOU FEEL ALONE
YOU'VE LOST YOUR LOVE
THINK KNOW IT ALL
AND THEN YOU FALL

KISS

AND WHEN YOU KISS
YOU WILL NOT MISS
THE JOY YOU FEEL
AND SO REVEAL
YOUR MOMENTS HIGH
AND WONDER WHY
IT ALL SEEMS STRANGE
MORE TO ARRANGE
EVERY NEW DAY
THINGS COME YOUR WAY
AND TEACH YOU HOW
TO NATURE BOW
WITH LIPS AFLAME

L

AND END THIS VERSE
WITH LOVE NOT A CURSE

LAZY

I AM SO LAZY
IT MAKES ME CRAZY
HAVE NOTHING TO DO
SIT AND THINK OF YOU
MAYBE YOU WILL CALL
THEN I WILL SIT TALL
HOWEVER RIGHT NOW
MY HEAD IN A BOW
I CAN'T EVEN THINK
DON'T FEEL IN THE PINK
I JUST WAIT AND WAIT
IT IS JUST MY FATE
IT MAKES ME CRAZY
I AM SO LAZY

LEAVING

PACK UP YOUR BAG
YOUR FEET DON'T DRAG
ITS COMING SOON
ANGEL AND GOON
GET OUT OF BED
AND USE YOUR HEAD
BEFORE ITS LATE
SO CHOOSE YOUR FATE
YOUR DREAM DESTROYED
YOU CAN'T AVOID
THE TRUTH IS HERE
ITS ALL SO CLEAR
SO COUNT THE DAYS
AND CHANGE YOUR WAYS
YOUR FEET DON'T DRAG
PACK UP YOUR BAG

LEARNING

HOW CAN IT BE
THAT I CANNOT SEE
THINGS CLEARLY IN FRONT OF ME
SOMETIMES I WONDER
WHY I ALWAYS BLUNDER
FINDING MYSELF DOWN UNDER
I REVIEW MY THOUGHTS
TAKE THEM TO HIGHER COURTS
THE YEAS AND THE NAUGHTS
I'LL COME OUT JUST FINE
WITH HELP FROM DIVINE
TASTING SOME GOOD WINE
WITH THESE FINAL WORDS
GONE ARE ALL THE TURDS
I FLY WITH THE BIRDS

LESS AND MORE

DO LESS AND LESS
OUT OF THE MESS
FREE UP YOUR SOUL
HEAR THE DRUM ROLL
FREE UP YOUR MIND
AND NO MORE GRIND
PRACTICE EACH DAY
JUMP IN THE HAY
NO DESIRE
NO BURNING FIRE
AND LIVE IN PEACE
WORRIES WILL CEASE
IT'S HARD TO DO
THE LIKES OF YOU

BECAUSE YOU NEED
TO FREE OF GREED
SO YOU WANT MORE
MONEY'S THE DOOR
AND SO YOU THINK
WITHOUT A BLINK
SOMEDAY YOU'LL STOP
BEFORE YOU DROP
BUT YOU'RE CONTROLLED
AND IN THE FOLD
DO WHAT YOU'RE TOLD
AND THEN GROW OLD
OH WHAT A MESS
YOU CAN'T DO LESS

LET THE LIGHT SHINE

LET THE LIGHT SHINE
LOVE SO SUBLIME
EVEN WHEN OLD
LOVE DOES UNFOLD
ALWAYS IN YOU
BECAUSE IT'S TRUE
NEVER FADES AWAY
EVEN TO THIS DAY
IT'S ALWAYS THERE
NO MATTER WHERE
YOU TRAVEL FAR
AND REACH THE STAR
IN HEAVEN'S BLUE
STILL LOVING YOU
LOVE SO SUBLIME
LET THE LIGHT SHINE

LIES

LIES LIES LIES
BECOME WISE

BECOME AWAKE
GOODNESS SAKE
LEARN THE FACTS
INSANE ACTS
NO CONTROL
WHAT'S YOUR ROLE
PLEASE DON'T SLEEP
ARE YOU SHEEP
YOUR SPIRIT
CAN HEAR IT
BECOME AWAKE
GOODNESS SAKE

LIFE

OH WHAT GREAT JOY
LIKE A YOUNG BOY
THEN I'M SO SAD
LIKE AND OLD LAD
ALL LIFE'S CHANGES
THROUGH ALL RANGES
YOU GO UP AND DOWN
SMILE AND THEN FROWN
AND WHAT'S TO COME
BITTER SWEET HAVE SOME
ONE DAY OLDER
ON YOUR SHOULDER
WHAT WILL YOU DO
MUST SEE IT THROUGH
LIKE A YOUNG BOY
FULL OF LIFE'S JOY

LIFE (2)

EVERY DAY I DO MY BEST
LIFE IS ALWAYS SUCH A TEST
EVERYTHING I DO
I THINK THROUGH AND THROUGH

NO MATTER HOW I TRY
I STOP AND WONDER WHY
SOME THINGS GO VERY WELL
OTHER THINGS I CAN'T TELL
HOWEVER ALL IN ALL
IT'S A PEAK AND A FALL
THIS IS NOTHING NEW
WHY AM I TELLING YOU?
YOU KNOW HOW LIFE IS
IT'S JUST LIKE SHOW BIZ
WIN SOME, LOSE SOME TOO
ITS ALL GOOD FOR YOU
THAT'S HOW YOU LEARN
AT EVERY TURN
THE ROAD IS WINDING
THAT'S WHAT I'M FINDING
WHEN IT WINDS TO AN END
THERE YOU WILL MEET A FRIEND
WHO'LL TELL YOU MANY THINGS
OF GODS ANGELS AND KINGS
SO ITS EACH DAY
DO IT YOUR WAY
BEFORE YOU SAY GOODBYE
YOU STOP WONDERING WHY!

LIFE (3)

ALL THE JOYS AND SORROWS
TODAY AND THE TOMORROWS
THERE'S ALWAYS SOMETHING TO DO
YOU ARE NEVER NEVER THROUGH
WHEN YOU FINISH THIS
YOU HOPE FOR SOME BLISS
AND WHAT DO YOU FIND
JUST ANOTHER KIND
OF THING THAT NEEDS YOUR CARE
YOU MUST BE EVERYWHERE
SO OFF YOU GO
HOW WELL YOU KNOW
THERE IS NO END

OF THINGS TO TEND
WHILE YOU ARE ALIVE
YOU WILL ALWAYS STRIVE
TO GET THINGS DONE
AND HAVE SOME FUN
LIFE GOES ON YOU KNOW
WHAT AN ENDLESS SHOW

LIFE GOES

WATCH LIFE GO BY
YOU LAUGH YOU SIGH
YOU SEE THE SUN
YOU SEARCH FOR FUN
LOVE YOU WILL FIND
IF YOU ARE KIND
THEN THE NIGHT COMES
THE SILENT DRUMS
YOU DREAM A DREAM
YOU PLAN AND SCHEME
YOU CHASE THE BUCK
AND A GOOD FUCK
AND WHEN ITS DONE
YOU THINK YOU'VE WON
YOUR ILLUSION
YOUR CONFUSION
AND THEN YOU WAKE
HAVE A GOOD SHAKE
YOU LAUGH AND SIGH
YOUR LIFE GOES BY

LIFE'S ILLUSION

LIFE'S ILLUSION
YOUR CONCLUSION
HEALTH LOVE GOLD FAME
ITS ALL YOUR GAME
PLAY IT YOUR WAY

DO WHAT THEY SAY
SUCH A BIG GAIN
AVOID THE PAIN
LISTEN TO SPIRIT
THEN YOU'LL HEAR IT
THEN FEEL YOUR HEART
A PLACE TO START
STEP BY STEP GO
WATCH YOUR LIFE'S SHOW
THEN YOU WILL KNOW
AVOID THE BLOW
YOUR CONCLUSION
LIFES' ILLUSION

LIGHT

SEE THE LIGHT
IN YOUR SIGHT
IT'S SO BRIGHT
IN THE NIGHT
IN DAY TOO
PART OF YOU
LIGHT OF HEART
IS YOUR START
THERE'S YOUR LOVE
THE SKY ABOVE
EARTH BELOW
TREES DO SHOW
OCEANS OF BLUE
INSIDE YOU
IN YOUR SIGHT
SEE THE LIGHT

LIGHT (2)

PHOTONS OF LIGHT
WITH GREAT DELIGHT
ALL CONNECTED

RESURRECTED
PEACEFUL AND KIND
LOVE THAT WILL BIND
SOULS TOGETHER
THE SAME FEATHER
AWAKENED MIND
THERE YOU WILL FIND
WITH GREAT DELIGHT
PHOTONS OF LIGHT

LIGHT (3)

LOOK SEE THE LIGHT
YOU'LL FEEL ALRIGHT
IT'S ALWAYS THERE
UNDER YOUR CARE
IT'S UP TO YOU
TO FIND WHAT'S TRUE
AND KEEP YOUR CALM
DON'T LOSE YOUR CHARM
LET YOUR LOVE SPREAD
TAKE IT TO BED
NEVER FEEL ALONE
NO NEED FOR PHONE
YOU HAVE YOURSELF
YOUR OWN GOOD ELF
IN MIRROR LOOK
NOT IN THE BOOK
THEN FEEL ALRIGHT
ENTER THE LIGHT

LIGHT HEART

PLACE TO START
OPEN LIGHT HEART
ENERGY RAYS
ALL YOUR DAYS
FROM ABOVE

SPEAKING LOVE
TOUCHING ALL
SUNS GREAT BALL
TOUCHING YOU
THROUGH AND THROUGH
SO YOU KNOW
GREAT LIGHT SHOW
OPEN LIGHT HEART
PLACE TO START

LIGHT OF LOVE

LIGHT OF LOVE
SUN IS ABOVE
RAYS SO BRIGHT
BRINGING LIGHT
IN YOUR HEART
A QUICK START
OF YOUR FIRE
TO INSPIRE
YOUR LOVE ANEW
NEVER THROUGH
SO YOU KNOW
HOW TO GO
SUN'S ABOVE
LIGHT OF LOVE

LIKE YOU

HEAR MY STORY
THERE IS NO GLORY
I'M JUST LIKE YOU
SIMPLE AND TRUE
BEEN UP AND DOWN
AROUND THE TOWN
LOOKING AT THE GIRLS
STRAIGHT HAIR AND CURLS
THINKING I KNOW

THE WAY TO GO
UNTIL I FOUND
I LOST MY GROUND
AND THEN GOT UP
REFILLED MY CUP
AND STARTED OVER
WITH GREEN CLOVER
SO CLOSE YOUR EYES
PRETEND YOU'RE WISE
AND SEEK NO MORE
WALK THROUGH THE DOOR
SIMPLE AND TRUE
I'M JUST LIKE YOU

LITTLE WARM HOLE

LITTLE WARM HOLE
TO HIDE YOUR SOUL
YOU GO INSIDE
DON'T LOSE YOUR PRIDE
IN AND THEN OUT
YOU SCREAM YOU SHOUT
YOU COME AND GO
WHAT A FINE SHOW
BUT IS IT REAL
OR JUST YOU FEEL
YOU SEE THE STARS
ROCKETS TO MARS
OPEN YOUR EYES
AND BECOME WISE
TO HIDE YOUR SOUL
LITTLE WARM HOLE

LIVE EACH DAY

LIVE EACH DAY
COME WHAT MAY
ENJOY ALL

FLY OR FALL
MATTERS NOT
COLD OR HOT
WET OR DRY
SMILE OR CRY
IT'S YOUR LIFE
CHILD AND WIFE
WAR OR PEACE
IT WON'T CEASE
COME WHAT MAY
LIVE EACH DAY

LIVE WITHOUT FEAR

LIVE WITHOUT FEAR
LIFE WILL BE CLEAR
EVERYTHING TRUE
BELONGS TO YOU
YOU SEE THE SKY
AND WONDER WHY
THE OCEAN TOO
IS PART OF YOU
ALL LIVING THINGS
THE BIRD THAT SINGS
THE YOUNG AND OLD
THE STORIES TOLD
SO HERE YOU GO
WATCH THE BIG SHOW
LIFE WILL BE CLEAR
LIVE WITHOUT FEAR

LIVING ILLUSION

LIVING ILLUSION
YOUR CONFUSION
YOU THINK YOU KNOW
AND TRY TO SHOW
YOU DON'T REALIZE

YOU'RE NOT SO WISE
THE MIRROR SHOWS
FROM HEAD TO TOES
AND WHEN YOU LOOK
YOU MIND HAS SHOOK
SO YOU AWAKE
A NEW BREATH TAKE
YOU SEARCH AND FIND
NEW KIND OF MIND
NOT WHAT YOU THOUGHT
WHICH HAS BEEN TAUGHT
YOU'VE BEEN MISLED
LIES YOU'VE BEEN FED
LIVING ILLUSION
YOUR CONFUSION-

LOOK

LOOK AT THE SKY
AND WONDER WHY
LOOK AT THE STAR
IT IS SO FAR
LOOK AT YOUR HEART
IT IS SO SMART
KNOWS WHAT TO DO
TAKE CARE OF YOU
THEN LOOK ABOVE
AND SEARCH FOR LOVE
AND YOU WILL FIND
NOT IN YOUR MIND
LOOK IN THE SKY
AND WONDER WHY

LOOK AROUND

LOOK AROUND
HEAR THE SOUND
UP AND DOWN

NO MORE FROWN
FULL OF JOY
LOVE'S NEW TOY
ALL IS GOOD
AS IT SHOULD
FEELING FINE
SIPPING WINE
SO YOU KNOW
LIFE'S GREAT SHOW
HEAR THE SOUND
LOOK AROUND

LOOK AT THE CLOUDS

LOOK AT THE CLOUDS AND SKY
TAKE TIME TO WONDER WHY
IN ALL ITS BEAUTY
DOING ITS DUTY
GIVING US OUR RAIN
NATURE HAS ITS GAIN
THE PLANTS BEGIN TO GROW
IN ITS SPENDER DOES SHOW
THE COLORED FLOWERS
WATERED BY SHOWERS
FEEDING ALL THE PLANTS
THE TREES AND THE ANTS
SO MAKE A GOOD WISH
AND PRAY IT COMES TRUE
CLOUDS ARE FEEDING YOU
IN THE SKY SO BLUE
STILL WONDERING WHO
IS BEHIND IT ALL
WHEN THE RAINS DOES FALL
LOOK AT THE CLOUDS AND SKY
TAKE TIME TO WONDER WHY

LOOK IN MY EYES

SO FAR TO ROAM
LOOK IN MY EYES
WITHOUT A POEM
FOR A SURPRISE
AND BY MY SIDE
SOMETHING UNKNOWN
THE OCEAN TIDE
NOT HOME GROWN
WATER SO BLUE
SOMETHING QUITE NEW
THINKING OF YOU
DESIGNED FOR TWO
YOUR WARM EMBRACE
WHEN YOU TRY IT
TOUCHING MY FACE
DON'T DENY IT
WARM SAND BELOW
A HIDDEN DREAM
WHERE MY FEET GO
IT MAY WELL SEEM
SUN ON MY FACE
SOMETHING SO STRANGE
I LOVE THIS PLACE
OUT OF YOUR RANGE
AM HERE ALL DAY
HAVE A GOOD LOOK
THIS IS MY WAY
INSIDE YOUR BOOK
WITHOUT A POEM
FOR A SURPRISE
SO FAR TO ROAM
LOOK IN MY EYES

LOOK INSIDE

LOOK INSIDE
FIND YOUR PRIDE

OPEN YOUR EYES WIDE
PLEASE DON'T TRY TO HIDE
DON'T PUT YOUR INNER SELF
FAR AWAY ON SHELF
TV ALL NIGHT
WATCHING THE FIGHT
COMPUTER ALL DAY
EARNING YOUR SMALL PAY
WHILE THE BOSSES CONTROL
TEACHING YOU YOUR NEW ROLE
FIVE MINUTES ON THE CELL
WITH YOUR STORIES TO TELL
EVEN THE CHILDREN WILL CALL
DON'T LET YOUR SELF-ESTEEM FALL
ADS POLLUTING YOUR MIND
THEY'LL SELL YOU ANY KIND
ALL TO GET YOUR MONEY
LAUGH THOUGH IT'S NOT FUNNY
THE MORE YOU LOOK OUTSIDE
YOU'LL LOSE YOUR INNER GUIDE
YOU MUST STOP AND THINK
DON'T LET YOUR SOUL SINK
WHEN YOU LOOK INSIDE
YOU WILL FIND YOUR PRIDE

LOOK SEE

LOOK AND SEE THE STARS
MERCURY MARS
AND DREAM YOUR DREAM
SO IT WILL SEEM
THE WORLD DOES CHANGE
IT'S ALL SO STRANGE
YOU TRY TO FIND
YOUR PEACE OF MIND
YOU'VE LOST CONTROL
DON'T KNOW YOUR ROLE
SO WATCH TV
AND THERE YOU SEE
ALL THE NEW STARS

AND SPEEDING CARS
AND SOME FAKE NEWS
GIVES YOU THE BLUES
SO WHAT TO DO
TO LIVE LIFE TRUE
LOOK AND SEE THE STARS
JUNIPER MARS

LOOKING FOR SOMETHING

WHAT ARE YOU CHASING
WHY ARE YOU RACING
WHERE ARE YOU GOING
IS THE TRUTH SHOWING
ARE YOU ABLE TO FIND
THE INSIDE OF YOUR MIND
ALWAYS ON THE GO
THINKING THAT YOU KNOW
HOPING TO FIND OUT
WHAT YOU ARE ABOUT
LOOKING HERE AND THERE
LOOKING EVERYWHERE
NEVER SITTING STILL
TRYING A NEW PILL
NEVER CONNECTING
NEVER REFLECTING
GOING ROUND AND ROUND
FEET NOT ON THE GROUND
LONG ENOUGH TO FIND
THE INSIDE OF YOUR MIND
WHAT ARE YOU CHASING
WHY ARE YOU RACING

LOSE YOUR FEAR

LOSE YOUR FEAR
LOVE YOUR DEAR

GIVE YOUR HEART
THERE TO START
YOUR SOUL TOO
REST OF YOU
LET ALL GO
THEN YOU KNOW
YOU ARE THERE
EVERYWHERE
ONE AND ALL
SO DON'T STALL
LOVE YOUR DEAR
LOSE YOUR FEAR

LOSING IT

WHAT A GREAT PAIN
GOING INSANE
AND BIT BY BIT
YOU'RE LOSING IT
CAUSE YOU DON'T KNOW
WHICH WAY TO GO
TRY AS YOU MAY
YOU'VE LOST THE DAY
YOUR LIFE ASTRAY
NOTHING TO SAY
GOING INSANE
WHAT A GREAT PAIN

LOSING MY MIND

LOSING MY MIND
MY HEART TO FIND
BRAIN IN CONTROL
SEEK MONEY MY ROLE
WHEN HEART COMES FIRST
LOVE IS MY THIRST
SO WHERE TO BE
I'LL LOOK AND SEE

I MUST DECIDE
LOVE OR MY PRIDE
I THINK I'LL CHOOSE
MY LOVE NOT LOSE
LOSING MY MIND
MY HEART TO FIND

LOVE

CRYING FOR LOVE
THAT'S ALL I'M THINKING OF
I DON'T CRY EVERYDAY
I THINK MY TEARS AWAY
I KNOW MY TIME WILL COME
I'LL EVENTUALLY GET SOME
I MEAN LOVE FROM THE HEART
I'LL HAVE A FRESH START
EACH DAY GOES BY
BUT I DON'T CRY
I JUST WAIT MY TURN
AND CONTINUE TO LEARN
IF I WAIT LONG ENOUGH
I'LL HAVE SOME GOOD STUFF
YES, I'M TALKING OF LOVE
THAT'S ALL I'M THINKING OF

LOVE (2)

LOVE MAKES YOU CRY
YOU WONDER WHY
A BURIED TEAR
YOU HOLD SO DEAR
BACK IN THE PAST
HEART PAIN DID LAST
AND NOW COMES OUT
A SIGH AND SHOUT
OLD MEMORY
INSIDE OF ME

THANK YOU SO MUCH
YOUR TENDER TOUCH
THE LOVE I FEEL
FOURTH CHAKRA WHEEL
SO DID IT SPIN
FROM DEEP WITHIN
YOU WONDER WHY
LOVE MAKES YOU CRY

LOVE AND FEAR

GIVE UP YOUR FEAR
LEARN TO LOVE DEAR
AND FREE YOUR SOUL
FROM THE DARK HOLE
LET LIGHT COME IN
THERE IS NO SIN
YOU ARE THE LIGHT
THERE IS NO FIGHT
IF YOU DO THIS
YOU WILL NOT MISS
SWEET AND WARM LOVE
SUN'S RAYS ABOVE
TOUCHING YOUR HEART
NOW TIME TO START
LEARN TO LOVE DEAR
LET GO OF FEAR

LOVE GENERATION

NEW GENERATION
FORM A LOVE NATION
WE'VE WAITED SO LONG
TO HEAR HEART'S LOVE SONG
PEOPLE MORE AWAKE
LIVE FOR GOODNESS SAKE
SEE SMILING FACES
LOVE ALL THE RACES

OH WHAT A GREAT THRILL
BY DOING LOVE'S WILL
MANY YEARS HAVE PAST
WE ARE HERE AT LAST
FORM A LOVE NATION
GREAT GENERATION

LOVE IS MY NAME

BEFORE I DIE
I WILL KNOW WHY
LOVE IS MY NAME
I HAVE NO SHAME
THERE IS NO BLAME
LIFE IS MY GAME
EGO NO MORE
OPEN NEW DOOR
SEE THE NEW LIGHT
LET GO OF FIGHT
ENTER VIBRATION
LOVING NATION
SISTER BROTHER
FATHER MOTHER
LIFE IS MY GAME
LOVE IS MY NAME

LOVE ME STRONG

LOVE ME STRONG
LOVE ME LONG
SING LOVE'S SONG
RIGHT NOT WRONG
SO I KNOW
HOW TO GROW
EACH NEW DAY
IN LOVE'S WAY
AND SO START
WITH MY HEART

FEELING GOOD
AS I SHOULD
LOVE ME LONG
LOVE ME STRONG

LOVE'S POWER

LOVE'S POWER
SPRING SHOWER
RAIN OF LOVE
FROM ABOVE
KISSES PLANTS
FEEDS THE ANTS
WATERS TREES
GIVES US DRINK
SO TO THINK
LOVE'S POWER
SUMMER SHOWER

LOVE WILL UNFOLD

LOVE WILL UNFOLD
THE STORY TOLD
THE WILD HEART
THE NEW START
WHERE CAN YOU FIND
THE VERY GREAT KIND
OF SUCH A FRIEND
SEEKING LOVE'S END
RIGHT HERE AT HOME
NOT FAR TO ROAM
OPEN YOUR EYES
YOU ARE SO WISE
SO LOOK AROUND
AND HEAR LOVE'S SOUND
THE STORY TOLD
LOVE WILL UNFOLD

LOVING

MAINTAIN INNER PEACE
ALL YOUR STRESS WILL CEASE
LOVE YOURSELF MY DEAR
THEN YOU BECOME CLEAR
AND THEN YOU WILL KNOW
WHICH WAY YOU WILL GO
WHEN CHOICES ARE MADE
NEW GROUNDWORK IS LAID
LOVE COMES TO YOUR HEART
YOU HAVE A FRESH START
AND FEEL THE NEW JOY
HEART BECOMES LOVE'S TOY
AND SO THERE YOU ARE
SO CLOSE AND YET FAR
FROM THE LOVE YOU ARE!

LEAVING

MY BODY IS DYING
MY HEART IS CRYING
MY VOICE IS SIGHING
MY SOUL IS FLYING
WHERE AM I GOING
THERE IS NO KNOWING
AND WITH THAT IN MIND
I HOPE I CAN FIND
THE COURAGE TO BE
AND THEN CLEARLY SEE
PLACE FOR YOU AND ME
UNDER THE BIG TREE
AND THERE WE WILL STAY
EVERY NIGHT AND DAY
MY HEART IS CRYING
MY BODY IS DYING

MANKIND

OH GOD WHY CAN'T THE WORLD BE GOOD
AND EVERYONE DO WHAT THEY SHOULD
SO MUCH SUFFERING AND PAIN
AND IT'S ALL IN VAIN
WHEN WILL MANKIND WAKE UP AND NOT
    DESTROY
WHEN WILL THEY TEACH EVERY LITTLE GIRL
    AND BOY
KILLING KILLING KILLING
EVERYONE'S SO WILLING
THEY HAVE ACCOUNTS TO SETTLE
AND THEY USE THE GUN METAL
IT GOES ON AND ON AND ON
SO WHEN WILL MURDER BE GONE
WE EACH DO WHAT WE CAN IN OUR WAY
WHY ARE REVENGE AND MURDER HERE TO
    STAY
WELL THAT'S THE WAY THINGS ARE
THE HEAVEN MOON AND STAR
SO I LOOK TO THE SKY
AND I STILL WONDER WHY
WE CANNOT STOP THE HATE
LOOKS LIKE IT'S STILL MAN'S FATE
SO NOW ALL WE CAN DO
IS BELIEVE IN YOU.

MEN ARE STUPID

MEN ARE STUPID
LOOK FOR CUPID
WOMEN ARE SMART
FROM THE FIRST START

THEY KNOW THE GAME
PLAY WITHOUT SHAME
MEN ARE ASLEEP
INNOCENT SHEEP
TOGETHER THEN
INSIDE A PEN
THE GAME THEN STARTS
THEN BROKEN HEARTS
FROM THE ASHES
AND SHORT FLASHES
THE GAME SOON ENDS
MAKING AMENDS
UNDERSTAND THIS
OR GO AMISS
FIGURE IT OUT
OR LOSE THE BOUT
IT'S TIME TO KNOW
IF YOU MUST GO
WAKE THE WALK
FORGET THE TALK
MEN WOMEN KNOW
IT'S ALL FOR SHOW
UNLESS THERE'S LOVE
THAT COMES FROM ABOVE

MARTIAL LAW

MARTIAL LAW
AT THE DOOR
WHAT TO DO
UP TO YOU
WAIT AND SEE
WHAT'S TO BE
IT'S ALL CLEAR
LIVE IN FEAR
JADE 15
IS THE SCENE
UN TROOPS
GET THE SCOOPS
SEE THE TANKS

CLOSE THE BANKS
DOLLAR FALLS
CLOSE THE MALLS
SO THEY SAY
IT'S THEIR DAY
AS YOU WAIT
BITE THE BAIT
SUCH BRIGHT FOOLS
YOU'RE THEIR TOOLS
SUCH GOOD SLAVES
ENDING DAYS
AT THE DOOR
MARTIAL LAW

ME

LET GO OF ME
THEN I WILL SEE
WORLD MORE CLEARLY
LOVE MORE DEARLY
I'M IN MY WAY
DURING THE DAY
BECAUSE I THINK
WITHOUT A WINK
ONLY OF ME
I CANNOT SEE
THE REST OF YOU
AND WHAT IS TRUE
SO I WILL LEARN
IT'S NOW YOUR TURN
FOR YOU TO BE
IN FRONT OF ME

MEN

YOU ARE OBSESSED
WITH WOMAN'S BREAST
SO YOU CANNOT REST

SO HERE'S A TEST
CLOSE YOUR EYES TIGHT
AND START TO FIGHT
THE URGE TO LOOK
CLOSE THE OLD BOOK
CONTROL YOUR MIND
AND HOPE TO FIND
A WAY TO PEACE
THAT WILL NOT CEASE
WHEN YOU LEARN THAT
AND START TO CHAT
AND FREE TO LEARN
ALL HAS ITS TURN
AND SEE CLEARLY
TREAT HER DEARLY
SHE IS YOUR FRIEND
UNTIL THE END
SO LET GO NOW
SHE'S NOT A COW

MENTAL CONTROL

MENTAL CONTROL
IS THAT YOUR ROLE
FEELINGS FORGET
WITH NO REGRET
USING YOUR MIND
THEN PLEASE BE KIND
TREAT THE GREAT TREE
WITH DIGNITY
AND BROTHER TOO
THE LIKES OF YOU
SISTERS ARE FINE
INVITE TO DINE
ON LOVE'S BIG HEART
SUCH A GOOD START
LEG TO OF FEAR
COME VERY NEAR
IS THAT YOUR ROLE
MENTAL CONTROL

MIND CONTROL

WIN VERSES LOSE
WHICH SIDE YOU CHOOSE
FIGHT EACH OTHER
FATHER MOTHER
WHICH IS YOUR TEAM
YOU LEARN TO SCREAM
SO PICK YOUR SIDE
PEOPLE DIVIDE
AND LEARN TO FIGHT
THAT YOU ARE RIGHT
THEY OWN YOUR MIND
THEY MADE YOU BLIND
RED WHITE OR BLUE
THEY SURE OWN YOU
YOU WATCH TV
AND THERE YOU SEE
TEAMS FIGHT EACH OTHER
SISTER BROTHER
OH PLEASE WAKE UP
DON'T WIN THE CUP
TAKE BACK YOUR MIND
THEN PEACE YOU FIND
WORK TOGETHER
BIRD OF FEATHER
COOPERATE
CAN BE SO GREAT
LET GO OF SPORTS
NEGATIVE THOUGHTS
LET LOVE TAKE HOLD
BEFORE YOU'RE OLD
OUT OF THE FOLD
MIND NOT CONTROLLED

MIND CONTROL (2)

MIND CONTROL
LOSE YOUR SOUL
FATE IS SEALED
TRUTH REVEALED
YOU AWAKE
NEW LOOK TAKE
THEN YOU FIND
YOU'VE BEEN BLIND
WATCH TV
THERE YOU SEE
ILLUSIONS
CONFUSIONS
ENTERTAIN
IS YOUR PAIN
ADDICTED
RESTRICTED
THOUGHTLESS NOISE
BUY THEIR TOYS
THE LATEST
THE GREATEST
YOU GROW POOR
THEIR STOCKS SOAR
IT'S YOUR ROLE
MIND CONTROL

MINUTES OF JOY

WHEN I MET YOU
THE LOVE POURED OUT OF MY HEART
I KNEW I HAD A NEW START
AND SINCE YOU FELT THE SAME
KNOWING IT HAD NO NAME
OPEN HEARTS WITHOUT SHAME
KNOWING IT WAS NO GAME
BOTH OF US IN THE SAME SPACE
OH, WHAT A BEAUTIFUL PLACE
THOSE MINUTES WERE SO SUBLIME

MOVED TO CREATE THIS RHYME
AND SHARE IT WITH YOU
KNOWING IT IS TRUE
FOR ALL THE WORLD TO TELL
INTO DEEP LOVE WE FELL
WHEN I MET YOU
I FELT LOVE THROUGH AND THROUGH

MINUTES PASS

MINUTES PASS
TAKE THE CLASS
NEED SOME MORE
AT GREED'S DOOR
NEVER ENDS
HAVE NO FRIENDS
FILL THE HEART
MAKE NEW START
CHANGE THE BRAIN
NO MORE PAIN
LIVE NEW WAY
EVERY DAY
WITH SUCH JOY
LIFE'S A TOY
AT GREED'S DOOR
NEED NO MORE

MINUTES PASS (2)

MINUTES PASS
GROWS THE GRASS
EACH NEW DAY
SUNS BRIGHT WAY
THINGS DO CHANGE
IN YOUR RANGE
FINDING LIGHT
MAKES LIFE BRIGHT
PEACE TO FIND

IN YOUR MIND
LESSONS NEW
ARE FOR YOU

MISTAKE

IF YOUR MISTAKE
FOR YOUR OWN SAKE
LEARN WHAT YOU CAN
WOMAN AND MAN
ADMIT IT ALL
AND NEVER FALL
STAY VERY TALL
CARRY THE BALL
AND WHEN YOU DO
RESPECT FOR YOU
SO THEN YOU LEARN
AT EACH NEW TURN
OWNING THE TRUTH
REMAIN IN YOUTH
FOR YOUR OWN SAKE
IF YOU MISTAKE

MONEY

EAT BREATHE SLEEP MONEY
IT'S NOT FUNNY
CORRUPTION LIES
IT'S NOT SO WISE
CORPORATIONS
DESTROY NATIONS
BUY THEIR TOYS
THEN LOSE YOUR JOYS
SO TAKE A STAND
LEARN TO FARM LAND
GROWN YOUR OWN FOOD
GET IN THE MOOD
NOW IS THE TIME

RID OF THE SLIME
IT'S NOT FUNNY
EAT BREATHE SLEEP MONEY

MONEY AND FAME

CHASING MONEY AND FAME
ARE YOU SURE THAT'S YOUR GAME
SOME NEVER HAVE ENOUGH
OTHERS HAVE IT SO TOUGH
THE CHOICE IS ALWAYS YOURS
IF YOU'RE SICK WHAT'S THE CAUSE
DO YOU NEED MORE AND MORE
DO YOU CREATE A WAR
WHEN DO YOU STOP
AFTER THE TOP
DOES IT GO FOREVER
YOUR NEW ENDEAVOUR
WHAT ABOUT THE POOR
WILL YOU BE UNSURE
ABOUT WHAT TO DO
JUST TAKE CARE OF YOU
ARE YOU AWAKE
FOR GOODNESS SAKE
WHERE IS YOUR HEART
WHEN WILL YOU START
OR WHEN WILL YOU STOP
DO YOU NEED A COP
CHASING MONEY AND FAME
ARE YOU SURE THAT'S YOUR GAME

MONEY OR FAME (2)

MONEY OR FAME
WHAT IS TO BLAME
IT'S HOW YOU THINK
SWIM EASY OR SINK
FAME IS FOR FEW

MAYBE FOR YOU
MONEY IS FOR SOME
IT'S HARD TO COME
SO THERE YOU ARE
WATCHING THE STAR
SEEING THE LIGHT
STRUGGLE AND FIGHT
IT'S ALL YOUR CHOICE
SAID THE SMALL VOICE
WHAT IS TO BLAME
MONEY OR FAME

MONEY AND POWER

POWER MONEY
RAIN OR SUNNY
EACH DAY THE GAME
YOURSELF TO BLAME
YOU MADE THE CHOICE
WITH SILENT VOICE
EVER CHASING
EVER RACING
YOU CANNOT STOP
MUST BE ON TOP
HIGHER HIGHER
DESIRE'S FIRE
STRONGER YOU GET
WITHOUT REGRET
UNTIL YOU FIND
LOST IN YOUR MIND
YOU CANNOT SEE
NEW WAY TO BE
YOU'VE SOLD YOUR SOUL
HEART BLACK LIKE COAL
A MONEY SLAVE
UNTIL THE GRAVE
BUT THERE'S STILL HOPE
SO LEARN TO COPE
OPEN YOUR MIND
TO SEARCH AND FIND

YOUR NEW WAY OUT
WITHOUT A DOUBT
IT'S NOT TO LATE
TO CHANGE YOUR FATE
AND BECOME FREE
ABLE TO SEE
NOT WHAT YOU THOUGHT
NOT WHAT YOU'RE TAUGHT
POWER MONEY
CLOUD OR SUNNY

KEEP ON GOING
IT IS SHOWING
IN YOUR FACE
ENDLESS RACE
NO CONTROL
OF YOUR SOUL
AND SO IT GOES
HEAD TO TOES
AT YOUR DOOR
MORE MORE MORE

MONEY SICKNESS

MONEY SICKNESS
IF I COULD BLESS
SOME OTHER THINGS
LIKE EAGLE'S WINGS
FIND A NEW WAY
TO START THE DAY
LOVE AND COMPASSION
I WOULD NOT RATION
SPREAD IT AROUND
A JOYOUS SOUND
BUT NO ONE CARES
THEY TAKE NO DARES
REPEAT THE SAME
AND TAKE NO BLAME
MONEY SICKNESS
OH WHAT A MESS
SO BLESS I DO
BY LOVING YOU

MORE

MORE MORE MORE
AT YOUR DOOR
WHEN TO STOP
THERE'S NO TOP

MORE AND MORE

NEVER HAVE ENOUGH
WANT MORE AND MORE STUFF
IS THAT WHO YOU ARE
WANT TO BE A STAR
FORTUNE AND FAME
IS THAT YOUR GAME?
MORE MONEY FOR YOU
BUT WILL YOU BE TRUE
WILL YOU SELL YOURSELF
YOUR SOUL ON A SHELF
THINK IT OVER WELL
OH HOW IT WILL TELL
IF YOU DECIDE
TO LOSE YOUR PRIDE
THINK IT OVER AGAIN
THERE IS NO TELLING WHEN
YOU WILL BE CAST ASIDE
AND YOUR FRIENDS WILL HAVE LIED
BEFORE YOU DECIDE
OPEN YOUR EYES WIDE
THE TRUTH YOU WILL SEE
YOUR FUTURE WILL BE
MUDDY OR CLEAR
SO HAVE NO FEAR
IT'S ALL UP TO YOU
WHATEVER YOU DO

MOTHER EARTH

MOTHER EARTH FATHER SKY
CAN YOU PLEASE TELL ME WHY
HUMANS HAVE MADE YOU CRY
MADE HUMANITY SIGH
WE HAVE CUT DOWN YOUR TREES
AND WE HAVE KILLED YOUR BEES
AND POLLUTED YOUR SEAS
AND HAVE SPREAD NEW DISEASE
SURELY WE ARE INSANE
TO PRODUCE ACID RAIN
AND TO CAUSE SO MUCH PAIN
FOR A FINANCIAL GAIN
IT'S TIME TO GET AWAKE
GIVE YOURSELF A GOOD SHAKE
AND TURN IT ALL AROUND
LISTEN TO NATURE'S SOUND
CLEAN UP THE PLASTIC SEAS
AND FEEL THE SUMMER'S BREEZE
AND START TO PLANT THE FOOD
AND GET IN A GOOD MOOD
PLEASE DON'T LOOSE ANY TIME
TO REREAD THIS SHORT RHYME
CAN YOU PLEASE TELL ME WHY
MOTHER EARTH FATHER SKY

MOTHER EARTH

IT'S ALL UP TO YOU
WHATEVER YOU DO
TO MAKE THE EARTH CLEAN
KEEPING IT ALL GREEN
AWAKEN OUR MINDS
IT WILL TAKE ALL KINDS
EACH OF US DO OUR PART
HELPING OTHERS TO START
WHEN YOU CUT DOWN THE TREES
YOU BRING EARTH TO ITS KNEES
YOU NEED TO BREATHE GOOD AIR

USING ONLY YOUR SHARE
THOSE WHO WANT MORE AND MORE
NEVER REACH THE GOLDEN SHORE
TO RECEIVE WHAT YOU NEED
PLEASE KEEP PLANTING THE SEED
OF FRIENDSHIP AND LOVE
KEEP THE BLUE ABOVE
NO MORE POLLUTION
IS THE SOLUTION
ALL OF US MUST DO WHAT WE CAN
REMEMBER HOW THE EARTH BEGAN
CLEAN AND PURE
THAT WAS SURE
IT'S ALL UP TO YOU
WHATEVER YOU DO.

MOTHER EARTH FATHER SKY

MOTHER EARTH FATHER SKY
ALL OF US WONDER WHY
HOW IT ALL BEGAN
THINKING ALL WE CAN
TRYING TO FIND THE CAUSE
TRYING TO OPEN DOORS
SOME SAY IT'S GREAT SPIRIT
OTHERS NEVER HEAR IT
COSMIC ENERGY YOU WILL FIND
GET KNOWLEDGE AND OPEN YOUR MIND
HEAL YOURSELF WITH PRAYER
DO IT EVERYWHERE
WHEREVER YOU GO
IT WILL ALWAYS SHOW
MOTHER EARTH FATHER SKY
IT'S SO EASY, PLEASE TRY

MOUNTAIN

MOUNTAIN HIGH
TOUCH THE SKY
SEE THE STARS
VISIT MARS
SEE THE MOON
COMING SOON
FINDING LIGHT
IT'S YOUR RIGHT
ALL IS CLEAR
NOW SO NEAR
KNOWING TRUTH
THE NEW YOUTH
TOUCH THE SKY
MOUNTAIN HIGH

MUCH TO DO

SO MUCH TO DO
THE LIFE OF YOU
NOTHING IS DONE
TO HAVE SOME FUN
GET MORE AND MORE
CAN'T SHUT THE DOOR
IT NEVER ENDS
SO MAKE AMENDS
BEFORE IT'S TOO LATE
IT IS YOUR FATE
YOUR FUTURE FIND
OR LOSE YOUR MIND
SLOW DOWN
FROM TOES TO CROWN
THE LIFE OF YOU
SO MUCH TO DO

MOURNING

GOD I ASK NOTHING FROM YOU
THAT WAY I CAN COPE WITH MY PAIN
IF EVERYTHING I BELIEVE IS TRUE
I WILL NOT HAVE SUFFERED IN VAIN
I MUST GIVE MYSELF A CHANCE
EVEN IF ITS JUST A GLANCE
LOOKING AT MYSELF AND EMOTIONS
THERE ARE NO MAGIC POTIONS
I CRY FROM THE HEART
AND WITH TEARS I START
EACH MOMENT OF THE DAY
HOPING THEY GO AWAY
EACH NIGHT BEFORE I SLEEP
AND INTO BED I CREEP
GOD I ASK NOTHING FROM YOU
AS I FACE EVERYTHING TRUE.

MY HEART

YOU TOUCHED MY HEART
WITH A JUMP START
AND NOW ALIVE
SO LOVE CAN THRIVE
I SEE YOUR EYES
A LOOK SO WISE
AS IF YOU KNOW
THE WAY TO GO
UP DOWN BACK FRONT
WHERE IS THE HUNT
OR NOT AT ALL
AND NEVER FALL
SO CAREFUL BE
THEN YOU WILL SEE
WITH A JUMP START
YOU TOUCHED MY HEART

MY HEART (2)

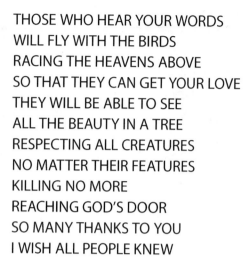

MY HEART CRIES OUT
MY VOICE WILL SHOUT
WORLD HAS GONE MAD
I AM SO SAD
SEEKING THE DAY
TRY AS I MAY
WHAT CAN I DO
JUST LOVING YOU
I LOOK AROUND
I HEAR THE SOUND
SYRIA WAR
OPENS NEW DOOR
FURGERSON FEAR
EBOLA NEAR
WHAT WILL COME NEXT
I AM PERPLEXED
DOLLAR KEEPS SHRINKING
I AM THINKING
I WILL STAY CALM
PLANT ON MY FARM
I MUST STAY REAL
LEARNING TO FEEL
PEACE IN MY HEART
THAT'S WHERE I'LL START
MY VOICE WILL SHOUT
PEACE WILL CRY OUT

MY LIFE

THANK YOU GOD FOR MY LIFE
MAKING IT FREE FROM STRIFE
IF I FOLLOW YOU ALWAYS
I'LL LIVE HUNDRED THOUSAND DAYS
I'LL LEARN THE LESSONS YOU TEACH
AND THEN I'LL BEGIN TO PREACH
SO THAT OTHERS MAY KNOW
WHICH WAY THEY NEED TO GO

THOSE WHO HEAR YOUR WORDS
WILL FLY WITH THE BIRDS
RACING THE HEAVENS ABOVE
SO THAT THEY CAN GET YOUR LOVE
THEY WILL BE ABLE TO SEE
ALL THE BEAUTY IN A TREE
RESPECTING ALL CREATURES
NO MATTER THEIR FEATURES
KILLING NO MORE
REACHING GOD'S DOOR
SO MANY THANKS TO YOU
I WISH ALL PEOPLE KNEW

MY LOVE

A WARM EMBRACE
A SMILING FACE
HEARTS THAT MEET
WHAT A TREAT
TO HAVE YOU NEAR
MY LOVELY DEAR
TO MAKE YOU REAL
MY LOVE TO FEEL
OH WHERE ARE YOU NOW
I'LL FIND YOU SOMEHOW
LOOKING HERE AND THERE
LOOKING EVERYWHERE
MORE THAN A DREAM
OUR LOVE WILL SEEM
TO BE SO WARM
YOUR LOVELY FORM
YOUR BEAUTIFUL EYES
YOUR GOOD MIND SO WISE
AS YOU APPEAR
I LOSE MY FEAR
OF NOT FINDING YOU
MY LOVE HAS COME TRUE
WITH YOUR SMILING FACE
AND YOUR WARM EMBRACE

MY SOUL

WHAT IS MY SOUL
IT MAKES ME WHOLE
I LOOK AROUND
IT MAKES NO SOUND
THEY SAY IT'S THERE
LOOK EVERYWHERE
I TRIED AND TRIED
AND THEN I CRIED
AND THEN BEHOLD
IT DID UNFOLD
AND NOW I KNOW
WHERE I WILL GO
I LOOK INSIDE
GIVE UP MY PRIDE
AND THEN I FIND
WITHOUT MY MIND
WHERE IS MY SOUL
THAT MADE ME WHOLE

MY WORLD

YOU ARE MY WORLD
MY LOVE UNFURLED
I SEE YOUR SMILE
ONCE IN A WHILE
THEN I FEEL GOOD
JUST LIKE I SHOULD
EACH DAY LOVE MORE
OPEN SOUL'S DOOR
AND THERE I FIND
SUCH PEACE OF MIND
AND THERE I STAY
PLEASE COME MY WAY
AND BE WITH ME
FOR CAN'T YOU SEE
YOU ARE MY WORLD
YOUR LOVE UNFURLED

NATURE

CLOUD AM I
IN THE SKY
CHANGING ALL
NEVER FALL
SEE THE TREE
HEAR THE BEE
MOUNTAIN TOO
PART OF YOU
OCEAN BLUE
HEART SO TRUE
FINDING LOVE
FROM ABOVE
IN THE SKY
CLOUD AM I

NATURE AND MAN

NATURE FEEDS ITSELF
NO FOOD FROM THE SHELF
MAN USES HIS BRAIN
AND MAY CAUSE MUCH PAIN
MAN MAKES EVIL MONEY
BEES MAKE THEIR HONEY
SO NOW STOP AND THINK
AS QUICK AS A WINK
WHERE YOU ARE GOING
WITHOUT YOUR KNOWING
AS SMART AS YOU ARE
YOU ARE VERY FAR
YOU CANNOT COMPETE
YOU'RE JUST A BIG CHEAT
WITH YOUR DESTRUCTION

NO REAL CONSTRUCTION
ONLY ILLUSIONS
YOUR FALSE CONCLUSIONS
SO IT'S WAKE UP TIME
LISTEN TO THIS RHYME
NO FOOD FROM THE SHELF
LEARN TO FEED YOURSELF

NATURE'S TURN

WIND SO CALM
SUMMER'S CHARM
BRIGHT GREEN LEAVES
ON THE TREES
THE BIRDS SONG
ALL DAY LONG
SILENT NIGHT
ALL IS RIGHT
DAYBREAK'S HERE
WITHOUT FEAR
SUN DOES RISE
EARTH SO WISE
SO WE LEARN
NATURE'S TURN

NEED SOME MORE

NEED SOME MORE
AT GREED'S DOOR
NEVER ENDS
HAVE NO FRIENDS
FILL THE HEART
MAKE NEW START
CHANGE THE BRAIN
NO MORE PAIN
LIVE NEW WAY
EVERY DAY
WITH SUCH JOY

LIFE'S A TOY
AT GREED'S DOOR
NEED NO MORE

NEVER ENOUGH

NEVER HAVE ENOUGH
WHAT MAKES YOU SO TOUGH
WANTING MORE AND MORE
MAKES YOUR MIND SO SORE
NEVER SATISFIED
OH HOW MUCH YOU CRIED
A FASTER CAR
TO TRAVEL FAR
NINETY MILES AN HOUR
THROUGH RAIN AND SHOWER
NEED TO GO FASTER
MAKING DISASTER
WHEN WILL YOU STOP
OVER THE TOP
STILL NEED TO GO
MAKE A BIG SHOW
WHY NOT LOOK INSIDE
DEVELOP YOUR PRIDE
AND YOUR SELF ESTEEM
AND THEN IT WILL SEEM
YOU ARE REALLY JUST FINE
NO NEED TO HEAD THE LINE
DON'T NEED TO BE SO TOUGH
YOU'LL REALLY HAVE ENOUGH

NEVER TOO LATE

NEVER TOO LATE
TO CHANGE YOUR FATE
YOU'RE BORN A SLAVE
DIGGING YOUR GRAVE
TIME TO REJOICE

AND CHANGE YOUR VOICE
AND CHANGE THE TUNE
AND DO IT SOON
THINK OF YOUR DREAMS
ALL THAT IT SEEMS
LOOK AT THE SKY
AND WONDER WHY
LOOK AT THE SEA
ALL YOU CAN BE
THE OCEAN TOO
IS GOOD FOR YOU
THUS NATURE RULES
AND SHOWS THE FOOLS
NEVER TOO LATE
TO CHANGE YOUR FATE

NEW WORLD

DECEPTION
CONCEPTION
NEW IDEA
NO MORE FEAR
TAKE CONTROL
LEARN NEW ROLE
TIME HAS COME
ALL NOT SOME
FREEDOM REINS
NO MORE PAINS
NEW WORLD FORMS
RID OLD NORMS

NEW WORLD BANK

NEW GLOBAL BANK
ALL MONEY SANK
RESET YOUR BRAIN
READY FOR PAIN
HAVE A DOLLAR

YOU WILL HOLLAR
MEDIA HELPING YOU
TURNING THE SCREW
YOU'LL HAVE NO CHOICE
YOU HAVE NO VOICE
SO SAY THANK YOU
IS ALL YOU CAN DO
HOPING TO THRIVE
AND STAY ALIVE
VACCINATION
ALL THE NATION
REREAD THE WORDS
THEY'RE NOT JUST TURDS
ALL MONEY SANK
NEW GLOBAL BANK

NEW WORLD PEACE

NOW NEW WORLD PEACE
ALL WARS DO CEASE
PEOPLE REJOICE
A HAPPY VOICE
A SMILING FACE
NEW HUMAN RACE
HELPS EACH OTHER
SISTER BROTHER
THE CHILDREN LEARN
EACH HAS A TURN
THEY PLANT THE SEEDS
AND DO GOOD DEEDS
THEY SHARE THE FOOD
LOVE IS THE MOOD
THEY SING AND TALK
THEY WALK THE WALK
ALL WARS CEASE
WITH NEW WORLD PEACE

NO BLAME

WE'RE ALL THE SAME
THERE IS NO BLAME
OPEN YOUR MIND
LEARN TO BE KIND
LOOK SEE BEAUTY
IT'S YOUR DUTY
CHILDREN MUST LEARN
ALL HAVE OUR TURN
SEE THE FLOWER
THE EIFFEL TOWER
THE RED RED ROSE
EVERYONE KNOWS
FEEL THE RAIN
WASH AWAY PAIN
LOOK AT THE CLOUD
AND THEN FEEL PROUD
TOGETHER ALL
WE'LL NEVER FALL
MOUNTAIN SO HIGH
WE WONDER WHY
THE WORLD IS SO
WE COME AND GO
THERE IS NO BLAME
WE'RE ALL THE SAME

OCEAN OF TEARS

OCEANS OF TEARS
WAR'S DEADLY FEARS
IRAQ'S GREAT PAIN
NOTHING TO GAIN
JUST LOOK AROUND
BODIES ON THE GROUND
HEAR THE BOMBS FALL
SCHOOLS MOSQUES AND ALL
WATCHING TV
AND THERE YOU SEE
FACES OF LIES
ARE NOT SO WISE
FORGET TO CRY
BREATHE A BIG SIGH
WAR'S DEADLY FEARS
OCEANS OF TEARS
WHERE WAS THE HEART
WHEN THIS DID START
AND WHERE WERE YOU

OH, GOD

OH, GOD, GOD, GOD
WHERE IS YOUR VOICE?
OH GOD, GOD, GOD
I HAVE NO CHOICE
I CAN'T WAIT ANYMORE
PLEASE, PLEASE OPEN THE DOOR
PLEASE LET ME IN
I'VE DONE NO SIN
I SEEK YOUR ADVICE
I HAVE ASKED YOU TWICE

SAY SOMETHING THAT I CAN HEAR
I WANT TO LIVE WITHOUT FEAR
GUIDE ME IN WHAT TO DO
THEN I'LL ALWAYS BE TRUE
I'LL LIVE MY LIFE WITH YOU IN ME
THIS WILL ENABLE ME TO SEE
EVEN IF I DON'T HEAR YOUR VOICE
I'LL ALWAYS MAKE THE PROPER CHOICE
OH, GOD, THANK YOU FOR YOUR SILENCE
CREATE A WORLD WITHOUT VIOLENCE
CREATE A WORLD WITH LOVE
WITH GUIDANCE FROM ABOVE
THEN WE'LL KNOW WHAT TO DO
IF WE DON'T HEAR FROM YOU

OLD

HOW TO GET OLD
IS NEVER TOLD
LET SILENCE REIGN
FORGET THE PAIN
JUST LOOK AROUND
HEAR THE WORLD'S SOUND
THE TOUCAN'S CALL
THE LEAVES THAT FALL
HEAR A DOG BARK
SIT IN THE PARK
RUN THROUGH YOUR THOUGHTS
THE YEAS AND NAUGHTS
THEN CLEAR YOUR MIND
EMPTINESS FIND
WHICH YOU CAN FILL
WITH A NEW THRILL
AND CLEARLY SEE
NEW WAY TO BE
IS NEVER TOLD
WHEN YOU GET OLD

ONE CANDLE

ONE CANDLE
BRINGS LIGHT
TO A DARK HOUSE
SO ALL CAN SEE
AND LEARN
HOW TO BE
WILL YOU LEARN
TO BE THE LIGHT
THAT ENDS THE FIGHT
THE PLACE TO START
IS THE LOVE
IN YOUR HEART

ONE SMALL WORM

ONE SMALL WORM
CAN EARTH TURN
HELPING SOIL
REDUCE TOIL
YOU TOO CAN
MAKE A PLAN
FOR A CHANGE
IT'S IN RANGE
DON'T WAIT MORE
END THE WAR
IN YOUR BRAIN
NO MORE PAIN
ONE SMALL WORM
CAN EARTH TURN

ONENESS

I AM PURE LIGHT
I SHINE SO BRIGHT
WE ARE ALL ONE
BRIGHT AS THE SUN
WITH ALL ITS BEAMS
REAL AS IT SEEMS
SO WE CAN SEE
THE WAY TO BE
USE OUR GOOD CHOICE
FROM INNER VOICE
INSIGHTFUL MIND
FOREVER KIND
UNDERSTANDING
NOT DEMANDING
AND SO WE KNOW
THE WAY TO GO
I SHINE SO BRIGHT
I AM PURE LIGHT
WE ARE ALL ONE
UNDER THE SUN

ONLY LOVE

YES, ONLY LOVE
LIGHT FROM ABOVE
SHINES IN US ALL
THE SHORT THE TALL
OUR RELATIONS
ALL THE NATIONS
THE TREES THE BIRDS
ANIMAL HERDS
THE EARTH THE SKY
WONDER NOT WHY
IT'S ALL SO CLEAR
LIFE WITHOUT FEAR
LOVE IN THE HEART
EVERY DAY'S START
WHEN YOU AWAKE
FIRST BREATH YOU TAKE
LIGHT FROM ABOVE
IT'S ONLY LOVE

OPEN MIND

OPEN YOUR MIND
SO YOU CAN FIND
THE THINGS TO KNOW
MAKE YOUR HEART GLOW
NORMS YOU OBEY
RUIN YOUR DAY
SO LEARN TO SAY
DO IT MY WAY
CLEAN OUT THE OLD
THE NEW UNFOLD
SO DON'T GROW OLD
LEARN TO BE BOLD
AND STAND YOUR GROUND
MAKE NOT A SOUND
BECAUSE YOU KNOW
NEW WAY TO GO

AND WHEN YOU DO
TO YOU BE TRUE
FEAR NOT THE THREATS
HAVE NO REGRETS
BECOME STRONGER
AND LIVE LONGER
SO YOU CAN FIND
YOUR OPEN MIND

OPEN YOUR EYES

OPEN YOUR EYES
AND BECOME WISE
BECOME THE LIGHT
IT'S YOUR BIRTHRIGHT
HAVE LOVE AND PEACE
ALL PAIN DOES CEASE
BE A BRIGHT STAR
STAY NEAR NOT FAR
FROM YOUR HEART'S LOVE
PEACEFUL WHITE DOVE
KNOWING IN YOUR MIND
ACTIONS SO KIND
THUS BECOME WISE
OPEN YOUR EYES

OPEN YOUR MIND

OPEN YOUR MIND
LEARN TO BE KIND
LEARN COMPASSION
THE NEW FASHION
TEARS IN YOUR HEART
IT'S YOUR NEW START
FROM TEARS TO LOVE
BLUE SKY ABOVE
AND SO YOU LEARN
IT'S NOW YOUR TURN
LEARN TO BE KIND
OPEN YOUR MIND

OUR TEACHERS

ALL CHILDREN OF THE WORLD
BANNERS NOT YET UNFURLED
THE FUTURE IS ALL YOURS
COUNTRIES SETTLE THERE SCORES
YOU MUST BE OUR TEACHERS
YOU MUST BE OUR PREACHERS
YOU MUST SHOW THE WAY
YOU MAKE THE WORLD STAY
TEACH THE POWERS THAT BE
MORE CLEARLY HOW TO SEE
THE THINGS THAT MUST BE DONE
HOW TO PUT DOWN THE GUN
TEACH THEM HOW TO TALK
TEACH THEM FREEDOM WALK
DIFFERENT AS THEY ARE
FROM LANDS VERY FAR
WALKING HAND IN HANG
AND FEELING SO GRAND
STATESMEN CANNOT DO IT
YES WE KNOW THEY BLEW IT
MAKE THEM LISTEN TO YOU
OR ELSE WE ARE ALL THROUGH
ALL CHILDREN OF THE WORLD
NOW BANNERS BE UNFURLED

OUR WORLD

WHEREVER YOU GO, WHATEVER YOU DO
REMEMBER TO ALWAYS ALWAYS BE TRUE
IF YOU DO NOT FALL TO GREED
AND MAKE SURE TO PLANT A SEED
INSTEAD OF CUTTING THE TREE
FRUITFUL RESULTS YOU WILL SEE
OUR PLANET YOU WILL PRESERVE
CHILDREN GET WHAT THEY DESERVE
GIVE THEM A CHANCE TO BREATHE
NOT GET ANGRY AND SEETHE
IF YOU DO THE RIGHT THING
BIRDS CONTINUE TO SING
IF YOU DO WHAT IS WRONG
BIRDS WILL HAVE NO MORE SONG
IF YOU CONTINUE POLLUTION
THERE CAN'T BE ANY SOLUTION
SO IT'S UP TO YOU
TO KEEP THE SKY BLUE
WHEN MORE CEMENT GOES DOWN
AND YOU INCREASE THE TOWN
DEVELOPERS GET RICH
BUT THERE'S ALWAYS A HITCH
YES A PRICE TO PAY
ON THE JUDGEMENT DAY
WHEN THE PLANET GETS SICK
YOU MUST REMOVE THE BRICK
LET THE EARTH LIVE AGAIN
THEN I'LL PUT DOWN MY PEN

P

PARTING WAYS

MY HEART IS BROKEN
AND I AM CHOKING
WITH TEARS IN MY EYES
AND VERY DEEP SIGHS
WHEN I THINK OF YOU
I GET SO BLUE
I KNOW THERE'S NOTHING I CAN DO
JUST KEEP ON LOVING YOU
NOW THAT I SEE CLEARLY
AND I KNOW REALLY
WHAT KIND OF PERSON YOU ARE
NOW THAT YOU'RE SO VERY FAR
SO I MUST GO THROUGH
THE END OF LOVING YOU.

PATIENCE

LEARN TO WAIT
IT'S YOUR FATE
HAVE NO CHOICE
SO REJOICE
TIME DOES PASS
GROW THE GRASS
PURE HEART KNOW
COME AND GO
WATCH LIFE'S SHOW
WIND DOES BLOW
SUN WILL SHINE
RISE DECLINE
IT'S YOUR FATE
LEARN TO WAIT

PATIENCE (2)

PATIENCE LEARN
IT'S YOUR TURN
IF YOU NEED
THEN TAKE HEED
SELF CONTROL
IT'S YOUR ROLE
IT'S YOUR TIME
HEAR THIS RHYME
IT'S YOUR CHOICE
HEAR THIS VOICE
IT'S YOUR TURN
PATIENCE LEARN

PATIENCE AND PEACE

PATIENCE AND PEACE
ALL TROUBLES CEASE
SO START TO LEARN
IT'S NOW YOUR TURN
TAKE LIFE IN HAND
IT IS SO GRAND
WHEN YOU KNOW HOW
TO NATURE BOW
AND UNDERSTAND
SKY SEA AND LAND
BIRDS AND THE TREES
THE ANTS AND BEES
EARTH AND ITS PARTS
AND HOW LIFE STARTS
WITH ENERGY
AND SYNERGY
YOUR TROUBLES CEASE
PATIENCE AND PEACE

PATIENCE LEARN

PATIENCE LEARN
WAIT YOUR TURN
CALM YOUR MIND
PEACE YOU FIND
WHAT'S THE RUSH
LEAVE THE CRUSH
ALL THE SAME
LIFE'S OLD GAME
BORN LIVE DIE
WONDER WHY
LAUGH AND CRY
WONDER WHY
WAIT YOUR TURN
PATIENCE LEARN

PEACE

CLEAN OUT YOUR MIND
PEACE YOU WILL FIND
STOP THE OLD GRIND
LEARN TO BE KIND
YOUR MIND OWNS YOU
LEARN TO BE TRUE
UNDERSTAND LOVE
BE THE WHITE DOVE
THERE YOU CAN START
EMBRACE YOUR HEART
HEART FILLED WITH LIGHT
MAKING LOVE BRIGHT
LIKE A BIG STAR
SO NEAR YET FAR
SO HAVE IT NOW
YOU CAN LEARN HOW
CLEAN OUT YOUR MIND
PEACE YOU WILL FIND

PEACE (2)

WHEN WILL I GET PEACE
WHEN WILL TROUBLE CEASE
EACH DAY SOMETHING NEW
WHEN WILL IT BE THROUGH
EVERY WAY I TURN
SOMETHING NEW TO LEARN
I TRY TO STAY CLEAR
TO LIVE WITHOUT FEAR
FACING EVERY DAY
A NEW WAY TO PRAY
PEACE I WILL OBTAIN
TO LIVE WITHOUT PAIN
ALL I HAVE TO DO
IS BELIEVE IN YOU
SO OFF I GO
TO WATCH THE SHOW
AND KEEP PEACE INSIDE
WITH NO PLACE TO HIDE
IF I STAY CALM
RECITE THE PSALM
THEN I'LL HAVE MY PEACE
AND TROUBLE WILL CEASE

PEACE (3)

PEACE IN THE MIND
IS GREAT TO FIND
HELPS YOU UNWIND
WHEN YOU READ A PSALM
AND LEARN TO STAY CALM
ATTEND NOT THE BOMB
FOREVER THEY FIGHT
IT MAKES YOU UPTIGHT
ALL THINK THEY ARE RIGHT
GO ON WITH YOUR LIFE
DO IT WITHOUT STRIFE
PUT AWAY THE KNIFE

TEACH ABOUT PEACE
THEN WAR WILL CEASE
HAVE YOUR RELEASE
YOUR WORLD IS SO GOOD
DOING WHAT YOU SHOULD
WHEN YOU LEAVE THE HOOD
A WORD OF ADVICE
MAKES YOU FEEL SO NICE
RELEASED FROM THE VICE
THEN YOU GET PEACE OF MIND
IT IS SO GREAT TO FIND
LEARNING HOW TO UNWIND

PEACEFUL

PEACEFUL TO STAY
IS THE BEST WAY
WHEN YOU LEARN THIS
DON'T GO AMISS
PRACTICE EACH DAY
DON'T GO ASTRAY
THEN YOU CAN FIND
PEACE IN YOUR MIND
BE YOUR MASTER
OR DISASTER
BECAUSE THE WORLD
WHEN IT'S UNFURLED
PRESSURES ON YOU
FOR THINGS TO DO
YOU MAKE YOUR CHOICE
WITH SILENT VOICE
AND YOU OBEY
EACH DAY BY DAY
IF YOU AWAKE
AND NEW ROAD TAKE
YOU HAVE A CHANCE
FOR NEW LIFE'S DANCE
IS THE BEST WAY
PEACEFUL TO STAY

PEACE LOVE TAKES OVER

PEACE LOVE TAKES OVER
LIKE FIELD OF CLOVER
LOVE GROWS AND GROWS
NOBODY KNOWS
THE PEOPLE'S HEARTS
HAVE BIG NEW STARTS
WAR IS SO SMALL
OLD POWERS FALL
PEACE LOVE TAKES OVER
LIKE FIELD OF CLOVER
ALL FLOWERS BLOOM
HEART'S LOVE WILL LOOM
BULLETS MELT DOWN
JUST BY YOUR FROWN
KISS EACH OTHER
LOVE YOUR MOTHER
YOUR FATHER TOO
LOVE INSIDE YOU
FEEL YOUR HEART BEAT
TAKE A FRONT SEAT
ENERGY FLOWS
EVERYONE KNOWS
THE TIME HAS COME
TO BECOME ONE

PEACE NOT POWER

PEACE NOT POWER
GENTLE SHOWER
RAINING THE LOVE
FROM HIGH ABOVE
FROM FATHER SKY
YOU WONDER WHY
HUMANITY
INSANITY
SEEKING POWER

NOT THE FLOWER
FROM MOTHER EARTH
FROM WHENCE OUR BIRTH
SUCH ILLUSION
IN CONFUSION
SEEKING THE GOLD
HORRORS UNTOLD
OIL AND MONEY
IT'S NOT FUNNY
SO YOU CAN START
LEARN YOUR NEW PART
PLAY A STRONG ROLE
MAKE IT YOUR GOAL
PEACE NOT POWER
IN LOVE'S SHOWER

PICK ME UP

PICK ME UP
FILL MY CUP
WITH LOVE'S WINE
THEN I DINE
KISS YOUR BREAST
AND THE REST
TOUCHING HEARTS
WHERE LOVE STARTS
FEELING FINE
SO DIVINE
THEN TO KNOW
I MUST GO
FILL MY CUP
PICK ME UP

PLANET

A MILLION YEARS
PLANET WITH TEARS
POLLUTE MY AIR
MY HEART YOU TEAR
MY SKY IS GRAY
NO LIGHT OF DAY
MANY OCEANS FILLED
PEOPLE NOT THRILLED
GONE IS MY SOIL
MY BLOOD YOU BOIL
PEOPLE ALL LIE
THEY MAKE ME CRY
THEY STEAL AND CHEAT
CHILDREN THEY BEAT
VACCINATION
RADIATION
IT'S ALL OVER ME
SO CAN'T YOU SEE
DO SOMETHING NOW
BACK TO THE PLOW
IT'S VERY LATE
SO CHANGE MY FATE
RESTORE MY LIFE
AND END MY STRIFE
RELIEVE MY PAIN
AND YOU WILL GAIN
A MILLION YEARS
AND NO MORE TEARS

PLANET DYING

PLANET DYING
PEOPLE SIGHING
POLLUTED AIR
NOT HERE AND THERE
IT'S EVERYWHERE
AND SO BEWARE
POLUTED OCEANS
DRUGS NEW POTIONS
THE SOIL GONE TOO
THE END OF YOU
AS YOU SIT AND WATCH
HOLDING YOUR CROTCH
AND THEM YOU BLAME
WHAT A GREAT SHAME
YOU ARE SO LAME
THEY PLAY THEIR GAME
AND AS YOU READ
THEY PLANT THEIR SEED
IN YOUR DULL MIND
WHERE THEY CAN FIND
HOW THEY CONTROL
YOUR VERY SOUL
CAN YOU AWAKE
FOR YOUR OWN SAKE
PEOPLE CRYING
CHILREN DYING

PLANT THE SEED

SO PLANT THE SEED
GIVE UP THE GREED
GROW YOUR OWN FOOD
GET IN THE MOOD
IT'S TIME TO CARE
TREAT THE EARTH FAIR
DON'T POLLUTE AIR
LOOK EVERYWHERE

AND YOU WILL SEE
NEW WAY TO BE
AND LOVE THE TREES
PROTECT THE BEES
POLLEN THEY BRING
AS THE BIRDS SING
WE ARE ALL PART
OF A NEW START
SO DO YOUR SHARE
TAKE UP THE DARE
GIVE UP THE GREED
AND PLANT THE SEED

PLANT THE SEED (2)

HURRY TAKE HEED
AND PLANT THE SEED
YOU NEED TO EAT
YOUR HEART TO BEAT
DEPEND ON YOURSELF
THERE IS NO ELF
FUTURE IS CLEAR
LIVE WITHOUT FEAR
SO GET PREPARED
AND DON'T GET SCARED
NOW IS YOUR CHANCE
ENJOY THE DANCE
HURRY TAKE HEED
AND PLANT THE SEED

PLEASE BE GLAD

PLEASE BE GLAD
DON'T BE SAD
ALL IS GOOD
AS IT SHOULD
SO REJOICE
WITH YOUR VOICE

LET LOVE SPEAK
GOODNESS SEEK
ALWAYS THERE
EVERYWHERE
OPEN EYES
LOVING SIGHS
DON'T BE SAD
PLEASE BE GLAD

PLOWING

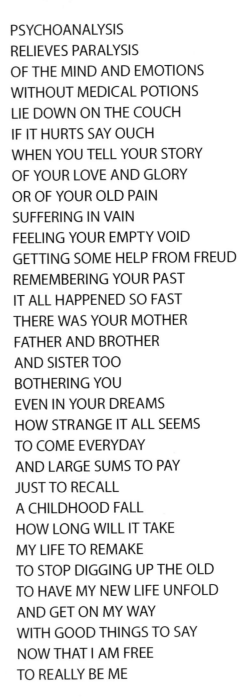

SO PLOW THE GROUND
AND MAKE IT SOUND
THE GMO
YES IT MUST GO
IT'S UP TO YOU
THINGS THAT YOU DO
DON'T KILL THE SEEDS
DO THE GOOD DEEDS
BACK TO THE SOIL
YOUR SWEAT AND TOIL
GO ORGANIC
GMO PANIC
EAT HEALTHY FOOD
GET IN GOOD MOOD
AND GET STRONGER
THEN LIVE LONGER
AND TAKE CONTROL
IT'S YOUR NEW ROLE
IT'S FOR YOUR LIFE
CHILDREN AND WIFE
THE TIME IS NOW
BACK TO THE PLOW

PSYCHOANALYSIS

PSYCHOANALYSIS
RELIEVES PARALYSIS
OF THE MIND AND EMOTIONS
WITHOUT MEDICAL POTIONS
LIE DOWN ON THE COUCH
IF IT HURTS SAY OUCH
WHEN YOU TELL YOUR STORY
OF YOUR LOVE AND GLORY
OR OF YOUR OLD PAIN
SUFFERING IN VAIN
FEELING YOUR EMPTY VOID
GETTING SOME HELP FROM FREUD
REMEMBERING YOUR PAST
IT ALL HAPPENED SO FAST
THERE WAS YOUR MOTHER
FATHER AND BROTHER
AND SISTER TOO
BOTHERING YOU
EVEN IN YOUR DREAMS
HOW STRANGE IT ALL SEEMS
TO COME EVERYDAY
AND LARGE SUMS TO PAY
JUST TO RECALL
A CHILDHOOD FALL
HOW LONG WILL IT TAKE
MY LIFE TO REMAKE
TO STOP DIGGING UP THE OLD
TO HAVE MY NEW LIFE UNFOLD
AND GET ON MY WAY
WITH GOOD THINGS TO SAY
NOW THAT I AM FREE
TO REALLY BE ME

PURPOSE

PURPOSE YOU FIND
WHEN HEART IS KIND
YOUR AIM IS CLEAR
YOU LOSE ALL FEAR
YOU GO AHEAD
HEAR WHAT IS SAID
YOUR INNER VOICE
YOU HAVE A CHOICE
LOVE ANGER JOY
PLAYING LIFE'S TOY
FINDING YOUR WAY
EVERY GOOD DAY
ITS ALL SO CLEAR
WHEN LOVE IS NEAR
YOUR HEART IS KIND
PURPOSE YOU FIND

QE3

QE3
WAIT AND SEE
DOLLAR FALLS
FED'S GOT BALLS
BUT NO BRAINS
CAUSING PAINS
ALL SUFFER
NO BUFFER
THEN BUY GOLD
DREAMS YOU HOLD
SAFE YOU FEEL
NOT MY DEAL
WAIT AND SEE
QE3

RAIN

WE NEED THE RAIN
TO GROW THE GRAIN
WATER FROM THE SKY
CLOUDS ARE SO HIGH
THEY HIDE THE SUN
WHERE WE HAVE FUN
WE WAIT FOR RAYS
AND SUNNY DAYS
BUT WE DON'T MIND
RAIN IS SO KIND
FROM RAIN WE DRINK
SO MINDS CAN THINK
IN RAINY DAYS
TO MEND OUR WAYS
TO GROW THE GRAIN
WE NEED THE RAIN

RAIN DROPS

RAIN DROPS ON MY HEAD
SILENCE NOTHING SAID
AS I WALK THE PARK
IN THE EVENING'S DARK
I CAN SEE THE BIG MOON
IN NATURE AM IN TUNE
THE STARS ARE NOT OUT
AS I WALK ABOUT
MOON GIVES OFF THE LIGHT
TO MY GREAT DELIGHT
RAIN DROPS ON MY HEAD
NOTHING NEED BE SAID

REALITY

REALITY
DUALITY
LIES CORRUPTION
WARS ERUPTION
THE WORLD ABLAZE
AN ENDLESS MAZE
HEADLINES ARISE
THE TRUTH OR LIES
WHAT TO BELIEVE
TRUTH OR DECEIVE
THE PASSIVE MIND
HAS BEEN SO BLIND
CHASING MONEY
WORLD NOT FUNNY
IT'S WAKE UP TIME
LEARN FROM THIS RHYME
LOOK FOR THE TRUTH
AND ASK THE YOUTH
THE WAY TO GO
CHANGE THE OLD SHOW

RELAX

TIME TO RELAX
PAY ALL YOUR TAX
YOUR MIND IS CLEAR
NOTHING TO FEAR
DO WHAT YOU'RE TOLD
AND DON'T BE BOLD
FOLLOW THE RULES
MADE FOR THE FOOLS
AND NEVER CHANGE
STAY IN THEIR RANGE
PAY ALL YOUR TAX
NEVER RELAX

REST YOUR MIND

LEARN TO REST YOUR MIND
FOR THEN YOU WILL FIND
YOU SAVE ENERGY
HAVE MORE SYNERGY
WITH INTERNAL PEACE
THEN CONFLICT WILL CEASE
YOU WILL FEEL THE CALM
BE IN NATURE'S ARM
AND THEN YOU WILL FLOW
WITH NO WHERE TO GO
AND STRUGGLE NO MORE
OPEN YOUR LOVE'S DOOR
WITH EVERY HEART BEAT
SO DEEP IN LOVE'S SEAT
FOR THEN YOU WILL FIND
HOW TO REST YOUR MIND

RESULTS

RESULTS ARE YOURS
FROM YOUR GOOD CHORES
THINGS THAT YOU GET
BY YOUR OWN SWEAT
SO NICE AND SWEET
THAT'S YOUR LIFE'S TREAT
THANKS TO IT ALL
AFTER THE FALL
YOU LEARN SO MUCH
THE GENTLE TOUCH
HIDDEN SOMEWHERE
IN LIFE'S BLANK STARE
SO YOU CAN SEE
THE WAY TO BE
FROM ALL YOUR CHORES
RESULTS ARE YOURS

RESTLESS MIND

YOUR RESTLESS MIND
CAN NEVER FIND
THE WAY OF PEACE
IDEAS CEASE
ALWAYS SEARCHING
BRAIN IS LURCHING
YET WANTS TO LEARN
NEW WAY TO TURN
TRY AS IT MAY
IN EVERY WAY
END IS THE SAME
NO ONE TO BLAME
SEEK AND CAN'T FIND
YOUR PEACE OF MIND

RICH AND POOR

ALL CORRUPTION AND GREED
WHILE FARMERS PLANT THE SEED
THE RICH WANT MORE AN MORE
STEAL FOOD FROM THE POOR STORE
THEY NEVER HAVE ENOUGH
WANTING MORE AND MORE STUFF
TAKING AWAY THE LAND
THINKING THEY ARE SO GRAND
KILLING THOSE IN THEIR WAY
NOT LETTING PEOPLE STAY
THOSE WHO OWNED THE LAND FIRST
NOW REMOVED IN A HEARST
HOW EVIL CAN THEY BE
WHEN WILL THEY EVER SEE
WE ALL ARE THE SAME
WHAT A GREAT BIG SHAME
THEY HAVE NO LOVE OR HEART
PLEASE WAKE UP AND START

PLEASE CHANGE YOUR WAYS
FOR BETTER DAYS
SEE ALL YOUR BROTHERS
FROM THE SAME MOTHERS
TREAT THEM RIGHT
STOP THE FIGHT

RUNNING

RUNNING RUNNING
OH HOW CUNNING
GOING NOWHERE
WITH YOUR BLIND STARE
SUCH ILLUSIONS
PURE CONFUSIONS
NO TIME TO FEEL
NO TIME TO HEAL
STOP LOOK AROUND
HEAR THE BIRD'S SOUND
NO TIME FOR LOVE
OR THE SKY ABOVE
MORE COLLECTING
LOVE REJECTING
AND SO YOU LIVE
LEARN HOW TO GIVE
RUNNING RUNNING
YOU'RE SO CUNNING

RUSHING

RUSHING ALONG
SINGING LIFE'S SONG
GOING SO FACT
EARTH IS SO VAST
YOU SEE IT ALL
BEFORE YOU FALL
SO YOU HURRY
AND YOU WORRY

YOU GO FASTER
FIND DISASTER
AND THEN YOU WAKE
FOR YOUR OWN SAKE
SLOW DOWN A BIT
TAKE TIME TO SIT
AND THINK CLEARLY
LOVING DEARLY
THOSE AROUND YOU
WHO ARE SO TRUE
SINGING LIFE'S SONG
WALKING ALONG

SAD OR GLAD

IS IT ALL SO SAD
WHY ARE WE NOT GLAD
STOP AND LOOK AROUND
SEE WHAT YOU HAVE FOUND
IS IT KINDNESS AND LOVE
OR BLACK RAIN FROM ABOVE
MORE CONCRETE OR TREES
BRINGS US TO OUR KNEES
CAN WE SURVIVE
AND STAY ALIVE
WILL IT BE WAR OR PEACE
WILL HATRED NEVER CEASE
NOBODY REALLY KNOWS
WHICH WAY THE WIND STILL BLOWS
MANKIND HAS A CHANCE
TO KILL OR TO DANCE
TO LOVE HIS BROTHER
OR LIE TO MOTHER
WHICH WAY WILL IT BE
WAIT AROUND AND SEE
WHO WILL STOP YOUR STRIFE
GIVE YOU A GOOD LIFE
DOES IT HAVE TO BE SO SAD
WOULDN'T YOU RATHER HAVE IT GLAD

SAVE THE WORLD

MY HEART CRIES OUT
I WANT TO SHOUT
PLEASE SAVE THE WORLD
AS LOVE'S UNFURLED
OLD DAYS ARE GONE

THE RANCH AND FARM
I FEEL THE PAIN
AS THE BOMBS RAIN
IT'S TIME TO STOP
BE A GOOD COP
PEOPLE MUST TALK
AND WALK THE WALK
DO SOMETHING NOW
TO NATURE BOW
SAVE ALL THE TREES
STOP KILLING BEES
TAKE BACK CONTROLS
BEFORE DEATH ROLLS
OH MY HEART BLEEDS
STOP EVIL DEEDS
FAST AS YOU CAN
WOMAN AND MAN
EACH DO YOUR PART
COME FROM YOUR HEART
I WANT TO SHOUT
LET LOVE ROLL OUT

SAVE YOUR BRAIN

PUT CELL PHONE AWAY
SAVE LIFE TODAY
RADIATION
OVER THE NATION
YOUR ADDICTION
YOUR AFFLICTION
COMPUTER TOO
OWNS ALL OF YOU
WE ALL ARE TRAINED
WE ALL ARE PAINED
THEY PLAN OUR LIVES
DESTROY BEE HIVES
AND BIT BY BIT
AND WHILE WE SIT
FREEDOM WE LOSE
THEY TURN THE SCREWS

WE SING THE BLUES
AND NEVER CHOOSE
WITH NATURE LIVE
AND OUR HEARTS GIVE
THE BREATH OF LIVE
TO CHILD AND WIFE
OH HOW I CRIED
MY BRAIN IS FRIED
AND NO ONE CARED
ALL WERE SO SCARED
AND NO ONE SHARED
AND NO ONE DARED
CELL PHONE AWAY
AND LIVE NEW WAY

SEARCHING

I LOOK HERE, I LOOK THERE
I LOOK EVERYWHERE
TRYING TO FIND
ONE OF MY KIND
WHO WILL UNDERSTAND
AND PLAY IN THE SAND
GET TO KNOW ME WELL
EVERYTHING, I'LL TELL
AND HOPE TO GET THE SAME
WHEN I REVEAL MY NAME
I DON'T ASK FOR MUCH
JUST A GENTLE TOUCH
SO WHEN WILL MY TIME COME
TO FIND THE LOVELY ONE
I LOOK HERE, I LOOK THERE
I LOOK EVERYWHERE

SEARCHING (2)

GOING HERE AND THERE
GOING EVERYWHERE

HOPING YOU WILL FIND
SOMEONE LIKE YOUR KIND
SEARCHING FOREVER
YOUR LIFE'S ENDEAVOUR
WHAT ARE YOU LOOKING FOR
WHEN YOU OPEN THE DOOR
HOPING TO HEAR IT
LOOKING FOR YOUR SPIRIT
WANTING TO BE WHOLE
AND FINDING YOUR SOUL
OR IS IT YOUR HEALTH
OR MORE AND MORE WEALTH
OR IS IT A MATE
TO MAKE YOU FEEL GREAT
OR A NICER CAR
TO TAKE YOU SO FAR
OR IS IT JUST FAME
ALL TO KNOW YOUR NAME
TO BE SATISFIED
AND KNOW THAT YOU'VE TRIED
ALL YOU REALLY NEED
IS TO PLANT THE SEED
AND THE YOU'LL KNOW
NEW WAY TO GO

SEE CLEARLY

IF YOU LIVE IN PEACE
LOVE WILL NEVER CEASE
THINK ABOUT WHAT YOU DO
MAKE SURE YOUR THOUGHTS ARE TRUE
WHEN YOU ARE CLEAR
AND HAVE NO FEAR
YOU WILL ALWAYS KNOW
THE RIGHT WAY TO GO
EACH MOMENT IN TIME
A BEAUTIFUL RHYME
BRINGING YOU JOY
ITS NOT A PLOY
IT'S VERY REAL

GOOD YOU WILL FEEL
FREE LIKE A BIRD IN THE SKY
AND YOU'LL NEVER WONDER WHY
LOVE AT YOUR DOOR
FOREVER MORE

NEVER GROAN
STRENGTH IS YOURS
OPEN YOUR DOORS
CLOSE THE DOOR
SEEK NO MORE

SEE THE LIGHT

OPEN THE DOOR
THEN LEARN SOME MORE
AND SEE THE LIGHT
NO NEED TO FIGHT
LIMITED BRAIN
WILL CAUSE MORE PAIN
NO LIFE IN VAIN
THE WORLD INSANE
CHANGE ALL YOUR WAYS
CREATE GOOD DAYS
SEE THROUGH THE MAZE
AFTER SUN'S HAZE
THE BEAMS THAT SHINE
NO NEED TO WHINE
LOVE IN YOUR HEART
THE WAY TO START
NO NEED TO FIGHT
HURRY SEE THE LIGHT

SEEK NO MORE

SEEK NO MORE
CLOSE THE DOOR
ANSWERS FIND
IN YOUR MIND
TEACHER HALE
ON LIFE'S TRAIL
HEAR THEM ALL
STAND DON'T FALL
YOU ALONE

SELF RELIANCE

IF YOU LOST DIRECTION
START SOME SELF REFLECTION
LET YOURSELF THINK AND FEEL
THE ANSWER WILL REVEAL
AS LONG AS YOU'RE ALIVE
YOU KNOW YOU WILL THRIVE
YOU WILL SEE THE NEXT DAY
MAKING A BETTER WAY
TO THINGS YOU WANT TO DO
YOU WILL SEE YOURSELF THROUGH
YOU ARE NOT ALONE
YOU DON'T NEED THE PHONE
YOU HAVE IT ALL
YOU WILL NOT FALL
YOU ARE SO STRONG
YOU'VE COME THIS LONG
SO ON YOU WILL GO
MAKING A GOOD SHOW
ONLY YOU WILL KNOW
HOW NOT TO FEEL LOW
IF YOU LOST DIRECTION
START SOME SELF REFLECTION

70 YEARS OLD

THANK YOU GOD FOR MY SEVENTY YEARS
I'VE HAD MANY SMILES AND LOTS OF TEARS
I'VE LEARNED A LOT ABOUT LIFE
NOW I CAN LIVE WITHOUT STRIFE
BECAUSE I KNOW WHAT TO DO

JUST KEEP LISTENING TO YOU
I'VE HEARD THE SOUNDS YOU MAKE
AND OF THEM I PARTAKE
THE SONG OF THE BIRD
SURELY THAT I'VE HEARD
THE DOG THAT WILL BARK
THE WIND IN THE PARK
I HEAR THEM ALL
THE WATERFALL
NOW HERE I AM BEFORE YOU
I HOPE THAT I DON'T BORE YOU
SO PLEASE DON'T GIVE ME ANY PRAISE
I JUST WANT MY SPIRITS TO RAISE
I CAN DO THIS ALL ALONE
WITHOUT USING A CELL PHONE
THANK YOU FOR COMING THIS DAY
SOON YOU WILL BE ON YOUR WAY
IT'S SO NICE TO HAVE A FEW GOOD FRIENDS
I'LL HAVE FIFTY MORE BEFORE IT ENDS

SHEEPS ARE WAITING

SHEEPS ARE WAITING
STILL DEBATING
LIFE IS FADING
TRUTH IS GRATING
YET NOTHING DONE
NO BATTLE WON
YOU WATCH TV
AND THERE YOU SEE
YOU'VE LOST YOUR BRAIN
AND LIVE IN PAIN
AND STILL YOU WAIT
TO MEET YOUR FATE
WITH YOUR CLOSED EYES
BELIEVING LIES
GONE IS SPIRIT
EARS CAN'T HEAR IT
YOUR CHILDREN PAY
YOU SIT AND PRAY

STILL DEBATING
YOU'RE STILL WAITING

SILENT PEACE

SILENT PEACE
WILL INCREASE
AS YOU GROW
THEN YOU KNOW
ALL WITHIN
WITHOUT SIN
IN THE HEART
IS YOUR START
THERE YOU FIND
WITHOUT MIND
LOVE IS KIND
THUS UNWIND

SIMPLE BE

SIMPLE BE
THEN YOU SEE
LOUD AND CLEAR
WITHOUT FEAR
EASY LIFE
LOSE THE STRIFE
BREATHE THE JOY
PLAY THE TOY
THEN YOU KNOW
IT'S JUST A SHOW
AND A GAME
WITHOUT SHAME
SIMPLE BE
COME AND SEE

SIMPLIFY

SIMPLIFY YOUR LIFE
LIVE WITHOUT STRIFE
TO NATURE RETURN
HAVE A LOT TO LEARN
BREATHE EAT DRINK AND SLEEP
GO BACK AND COUNT SHEEP
IN THE DAYS OF OLD
AND SO IT WAS TOLD
LET GO OF THE PHONE
LEARN TO STOP YOUR GROAN
AND INTERNET TOO
AND FIND A NEW YOU
IMAGINE NEW WAYS
ARE FILLING YOUR DAYS
WITH PLANTING THE SEED
LEARNING A NEW CREED
YES SIMPLIFY NOW
AND TO NATURE BOW!

SING

SING THE SONG
DO IT LONG
SING OF JOY
OF LOVE'S TOY
ENJOY LIFE
LOVE YOUR WIFE
SEE HER EYES
SHE'S SO WISE
KNOWS THE WAY
EVERYDAY
SO YOU FIND
LOVING KIND
DO IT LONG
SING THE SONG

SIT AND THINK

YOU SIT AND THINK
QUICK AS A WINK
YOU LAZY FOOL
JUST SIT AND DROOL
THEN YOU GET UP
DOWN COFFEE CUP
AND WALK AROUND
YOU HEAR A SOUND
AND THEN YOU FIND
YOU WERE SO BLIND
TO ALL THEIR GAMES
WITH MANY NAMES
YOU THINK SOME MORE
WHERE IS THE DOOR
AND THEN YOU SHOUT
PLEASE LET ME OUT
THE JAIL I'M IN
OH WHAT A SIN
TO LIVE AS DEAD
CLOSED MIND AND HEAD
CAN'T STAND THE STINK
I SIT AND THINK

SIT AND WAIT

SIT AND WAIT
SEAL YOUR FATE
CLOSE YOUR MIND
KEY CAN'T FIND
DUMB AND BLIND
NOT YOUR KIND
YOU LOOK FREE
YOU AND ME
CAN'T YOU SEE
WHERE YOU'LL BE
IT'S YOUR FATE
WAIT AND WAIT

SITTING STILL

SITTING STILL
USE YOUR WILL
DEEP IN THOUGHT
ALL IS TAUGHT
LOOK INSIDE
BE YOUR GUIDE
THERE YOU FIND
YOUR OWN MIND
ANSWERS NEW
INSIDE YOU
EVERYDAY
FIND YOUR WAY
USE YOUR WILL
SITTING STILL

SLAVE OF DESIRE

SLAVE OF DESIRE
PUT OUT YOUR FIRE
YOU'VE LOST CONTROL
YOU'VE LOST YOUR SOUL
CHASE ILLUSION
SUCH CONFUSION
NEW ONE EACH DAY
YOU PAVE THE WAY
WITHOUT KNOWING
WHERE YOU'RE GOING
FROM A TO B
YOU FAIL TO SEE
YOUR LOST SPIRIT
YOU CAN'T HEAR IT
AS YOU RESIST
AND YOU INSIST
YOU WANT DESIRE
YOU LOVE YOUR FIRE

SLAVES

WAKE UP YOU SLAVES
OUT OF YOUR GRAVES
WHY CAN'T YOU SEE
A NEW WAY TO BE
BURIED IN YOUR MIND
YOU CANNOT FIND
SOME NEW IDEAS
LIVE IN YOUR FEARS
YOU JUST COMPLAIN
MAKES YOU INSANE
LIKE RAT IN MAZE
VISION A HAZE
YOU JUST REPEAT
YOU EVEN CHEAT
YOU TELL THE LIES
YOU THINK YOU'RE WISE
YOU'RE STILL ASLEEP
YOU CREEP AND CREEP
TO GET YOUR GOAL
YOU LOST YOUR SOUL
SO LISTEN NOW
RESPECT THE TAO
OPEN YOUR HEART
TRY A NEW START
STUDY REAL LIFE
LET GO OF STRIFE
LEARN YOU CAN BE
LEARN TO BE FREE
OUT OF YOUR GRAVES
AND NO MORE SLAVES

SLAVES AND FOOLS

THE SLAVES AND FOOLS
FOLLOW THE RULES
THEY NEVER THINK
THEY SINK AND SINK
THEY LACK IDEAS
LIVE IN THEIR FEARS
THEIR MINDS ARE CLOSED
LIVE IN NEAT ROWS
DO WHAT THEY'RE TOLD
FOLLOW THE MOLD
AND ALL THE NORMS
AND ALL THE FORMS
WHAT A GREAT SHAME
THEY TRY TO BLAME
THEY LACK INSIGHT
AND THINK THEY'RE RIGHT
THE SLAVES AND FOOLS
FOLLOW THE RULES

SLEEP

TONIGHT WHEN I WENT TO BED
GOD WAS IN MY HEAD
IT WAS A NEW GOOD THOUGHT
A LESSON GOD TAUGHT
I KNEW I WOULD SLEEP SO WELL
FOR GOD DID TELL
HOPING FOR A HAPPY WORD
FROM GOD IT WAS HEARD
SO NOW I KNOW WHERE TO GO
GOD DOES ALWAYS SHOW
BEST WAY TO DO A THING
IS FLYING ON GOD'S WING.

SLEEPING WORLD

SLEEPING WORLD
LIES UNFURLED
FALSE NATION
KNOWLEDGE RATION
MANY MISLED
DON'T USE HEAD
ADDICTED
CONVICTED
DRUGGED ON PILLS
FEELING CHILLS
SOON AWAKE
LIFE'S NEW TAKE
LIES UNFURLED
SLEEPING WORLD

SMART PHONE

GREAT WORLD OF NOISE
AND DEADLY TOYS
YOU'RE ADDICTED
AS PREDICTED
YOU CAN'T LET GO
YOU'RE IN THE SHOW
THEY PULL THE STRING
YOU LEARN TO SING
YOUR THUMBS ARE NUMB
YOU'VE BECOME DUMB
IT DOES NOT MATTER
YOUR BRAIN DID SHATTER
YOU CANNOT TALK
YOU WALK THEIR WALK
IT'S NEAR YOUR BED
CLOSE TO YOUR HEAD
YOU HAVE NO DREAD
YOU'LL SOON BE DEAD
ALL THE NATION
RADIATION

SUCH DEADLY TOYS
GREAT WORD OF NOISE

SMILE

I LOVE YOUR SMILE
KEEP IT A WHILE
I LOVE TO SEE
WHEN YOU AND ME
ARE TOGETHER
BIRDS OF A FEATHER
FLYING SO HIGH
WE'LL NEVER DIE
SUCH IS OUR LOVE
ALL MADE ABOVE
YOUR FACE I SEE
IT TICKLES ME
KEEP IT A WHILE
I LOVE YOUR SMILE

SO EASY

IT'S SO GREAT
TO CREATE.
I PICK UP MY PEN
EVERY NOW AND THEN.
I LET THE WORDS FLOW
WHEREVER THEY GO
AND I MAKE A RHYME
EVERY SINGLE TIME.

SO REJOICE

TIME DOES PASS
GROW THE GRASS
PURE HEART KNOW
COME AND GO

WATCH LIFE'S SHOW
WIND DOES BLOW
SUN WILL SHINE
RISE DECLINE
IT'S YOUR FATE
LEARN TO WAIT

SOMETHING GOOD

BELIEVE IN SOMETHING GOOD
YES, DOING WHAT YOU SHOULD
THINKING THAT IT WILL WORK
HOPING YOU'RE NOT A JERK
TRYING EVER SO HARD
AND PLAYING THE RIGHT CARD
TILL YOU FIND THE WAY
HOPING LUCK WILL STAY
THEN LIFE TAKES ITS TURN
SOMETHING NEW TO LEARN
A NEW LESSON FOR YOU
TURNS THE ROSES TO BLUE
AND YOU THINK WHAT TO DO
TO MAKE YOUR DREAM COME TRUE
YOU START OVER AGAIN
YOU ARE WONDERING WHEN
SOMETHING GOOD WILL SHOW
KNOW THE WAY TO GO
AND HOPING IT WILL STAY
FOREVER AND A DAY

SOUL

WHERE IS YOUR SOUL
WHAT IS YOUR ROLE
WHERE IS YOUR HEART
WHEN DO YOU START
WHAT DO YOU THINK
WHAT IS THE LINK

ARE YOU ALONE
WITH YOUR SMART PHONE
WHERE IS YOUR FRIEND
HOW DOES IT END
IS LOVE YOUR GUIDE
OR DO YOU HIDE
ARE YOU CONFUSED
HAVE YOU REFUSED
TO THINK CLEARLY
TO LOVE DEARLY
SO STOP AND LOOK
INSIDE YOUR BOOK
WHAT IS YOUR ROLE
WHERE IS YOUR SOUL

SOUL (2)

REMEMBER YOUR SOUL
IT MAKES BODY WHOLE
IT RESTS DEEP INSIDE
SOMETIMES IT WILL HIDE
BUT IT'S ALWAYS THERE
SEARCHING IT, OH WHERE
THEN IT SHOWS ITS FACE
WHEN YOU SLOW THE PACE
HOW NICE IT CAN BE
AWAKE AND THEN SEE
YOUR SOUL IS SO GOOD
DOING WHAT IT SHOULD
IT MAKES BODY WHOLE
REMEMBER YOUR SOUL

SPEAK LOVE

SPEAK LOVE TO ME
SO I CAN SEE
SO MY SOUL LIVES
AND MY HEART GIVES

THE LOVE YOU NEED
AND PLANT THE SEED
OF LIFE IN YOU
FOR I AM TRUE
MY HEART IS YOURS
WITH OPEN DOORS
ENERGY FLOWS
FROM HEAD TO TOES
EVERYONE KNOWS
SPEAK LOVE TO ME
SO I CAN SEE

SPEAK TO ME

SPEAK TO ME
I LOVE THEE
WE CAN SEE
ALL THAT BE
IN WORLD WIDE
BY YOUR SIDE
UPS AND DOWNS
ALL THE SOUNDS
IT'S ALL THERE
EVERYWHERE
LOOK NO MORE
OPEN THE DOOR
I LOVE THEE
SPEAK TO ME

SPIRIT

WHERE IS SPIRIT
I CAN'T HEAR IT
IT CAN'T BE SEEN
RED OR GREEN
WHERE CAN I LOOK
NOT IN A BOOK
TRIED INTERNET

NOT A GOOD BET
I WENT TO SCHOOL
I WAS A FOOL
LOOKED HIGH AND LOW
SPIRIT NO SHOW
SO THEN IT GAME
I LEARNED THE GAME
I NOW HEAR IT
FOUND MY SPIRIT

AND MAKING A BIG SHOW
DOES NOT OPEN YOUR HEART
THAT'S WHERE YOU NEED TO START
SO LET YOURSELF FEEL
SPIRIT WILL REVEAL
YOU WON'T NEED TO LOOK
OR STEAL LIKE A CROOK
BE YOURSELF AND KNOW
YOUR SPIRIT WILL GROW
IT'S HERE IN FRONT OF YOU
ONLY WHEN YOU ARE TRUE

SPIRIT (2)

SEEKING THE SPIRIT
LISTEN AND HEAR IT
IT'S ALL AROUND
THE SILENT SOUND
IT'S ALWAYS THERE
NO NEED TO STARE
YOU HAVE GOOD EYES
THEY MAKE YOU WISE
LISTEN TO HEART
HURRY AND START

SPIRITUAL HEART

THE EGO MIND
IS NOT SO KIND
IT'S ONLY ME
AND NEVER THEE
WHAT CAN WE DO
GO BEYOND YOU
TO UNDERSTAND
SPIRIT SO GRAND
HEART AND SPIRIT
PLEASE DON'T FEAR IT
LET GO MIND'S FEAR
AS YOU COME NEAR
SPIRITUAL HEART

SPIRIT (3)

WHERE IS THE SPIRIT
IF YOU CAN HEAR IT
STOP AND LISTEN
IT WILL GLISEN
WHEN YOU USE YOUR EYES
YOU WILL BECOME WISE
AND ABLE TO SEE
THE BEST WAY TO BE
YOU WILL KNOW WHAT'S RIGHT
AND NO LONGER FIGHT
FOR HAVING SO MUCH MORE
DOESN'T OPEN THE DOOR
TO WHERE YOU NEED TO GO

SPIRITUAL LIGHT

SPIRITUAL LIGHT
DO WHAT IS RIGHT
NO NEED TO FIGHT
PEACE IS IN SIGHT
OLD WORLD OF FEARS
ONLY BRING TEARS
OPEN YOUR HEART
THE PLACE TO START

OPEN YOUR EYES
AND BECOME WISE
OPEN YOUR MIND
LEARN TO BE KIND
NEW WORLD AWAKE
NEW LIFE TO TAKE
DO WHAT IS RIGHT
SPIRITUAL LIGHT

START SEEING
START BEING
START LOOKING
WHAT'S COOKING

STARS

WATCH THE STARS
LOOK AT MARS
DREAM YOUR DREAMS
STRANGE IT SEEMS
WHEN YOU FIND
A NEW MIND
YOU'RE AWAKE
NEW VIEW TAKE
IT'S ALL CHANGED
REARRANGED
SUCH SURPRISE
IN YOUR EYES
LOOK AT MARS
COUNT THE STARS

STOP

STOP THE RUNNING
AND START SUNNING
CAN YOU SIT STILL
YOUR MIND NOT FILL
SO MAKE YOUR CHOICE
WITH SILENT VOICE
BE YOUR OWN FRIEND
AND LOVE YOU SEND
SO YOU AWAKE
FOR YOUR OWN SAKE
THE WORLD GOES BY
YOU SMILE OR SIGH
YOU WONDER WHY
IT'S ALL A LIE
IT MATTERS NOT
TAKE YOUR BEST SHOT
AND START SUNNING
STOP THE RUNNING

STOP

STOP SEARCHING
STOP LURCHING
STOP LOOKING
STOP BOOKING
STOP THINKING
STOP SINKING
STOP MOANING
STOP GROANING
START LIVING
START GIVING

STOP KILLING

STOP KILLING
GOD'S WILLING
IT'S CHILLING
NOT THRILLING
CHANGE THE GOAL
HAVE NEW ROLE
FEED YOUR SOUL
BECOME WHOLE
FIND NEW WAY
SAVE THE DAY

PRESERVE LIFE
END THE STRIFE
GOD'S WILLING
STOP KILLING

STOP THE BOMB

WHEN YOU STOP THE BOMB
AND WORK ON THE FARM
WAR WILL CEASE
WE'LL HAVE PEACE
WHEN WE ARE AWAKE
THE FIRST STEP WE'LL TAKE
SO HURRY HURRY
AND STOP THE WORRY
BEFORE ITS TO LATE
AND WE SEE OUR FAITE
TAKE ACTION NOW
AND WORK THE PLOW
PLANT THE SEEDS
WITH GOOD DEEDS
DO YOUR PART
WITH YOUR HEART
AND YOU WILL FIND
SOME PEACE OF MIND
WHEN YOU STOP THE BOMB
AND WORK ON THE FARM

STOP THE TALK

STOP THE TALK
START THE WALK
WORLD AFLAME
IT'S NO GAME
BIG MASS GRAVES
LIVING SLAVES
USELESS TEARS
ENDLESS FEARS

CHEMTRAIL HIGH
FILL THE SKY
AS YOU SLEEP
COUNTING SHEEP
START THE WALK
STOP THE TALK

STOP THE WAR

EVERYTHING HAS A PLACE
IN THE NO MAN RACE
BUT WHEN IT COMES TO SUICIDE BOMBERS
BETTER TELL THEM TO BECOME FARMERS
IF THE WAR COULD CEASE
WAKE UP AND HAVE PEACE
ISRAEL AND PALESTINE
ALL COULD BE DOING FINE
WHAT IS DONE IS DONE
PLEASE PUT DOWN THE GUN
IT IS TIME TO PLANT SEEDS
AND START DOING GOOD DEEDS
LET YOUR GOD HELP YOU AWAKE
OF GOOD DEEDS START TO PARTAKE
START THIS TODAY
CHANGING YOUR WAY
TEACH OUR CHILDREN TO LOVE
SEE THE HEAVEN ABOVE
AND START A NEW LIFE
WITHOUT THIS OLD STRIFE
SO THAT YOU MAY LIVE IN PEACE
THEN LET YOUR PEOPLE INCREASE

STOP TO THINK

WHEN DO YOU STOP TO THINK
HAPPENS QUICK AS A WINK
AND THE MOMENT PASSES
SO PUT ON YOUR GLASSES

LOOK THE MATTER OVER
IN A FIELD OF CLOVER
AND SEE THE HEALTHY GREEN
WHAT A BEAUTIFUL SCENE
LOOK AT THE OTHER SIDE
AND THEN YOU CAN DECIDE
THE THINGS YOU WANT TO DO
MAKING SURE YOU ARE TRUE
TO YOURSELF ABOVE ALL
SO YOU DON'T TAKE A FALL
HOWEVER IF YOU DO
DON'T STAY DOWN AND GET BLUE
GET RIGHT BACK ON YOUR FEET
THE NEW DAY YOU WILL GREET
WITH A CLEAN AND FRESH MIND
AND A HEART THAT IS KIND
TO EVERYONE INVOLVED
THE PROBLEM IS DISSOLVED
ALWAYS THINK IT OVER
IN A FIELD OF CLOVER

T

TAKE A BOW

STAND UP NOW
TAKE A BOW
WHO YOU ARE
COME SO FAR
DID IT ALL
UP FROM FALL
COURAGE NEW
GIVEN YOU
HOW TO LIVE
MORE TO GIVE
LEAD THE WAY
EACH NEW DAY
TAKE A BOW
STAND UP NOW

TALKING AND WALKING

STOP THE TALKING
AND START WALKING
WASTING YOUR TIME
BELIEVING CRIME
WATCHING TV
AND THERE YOU SEE
ALL THE FAKE NEWS
TURNING THE SCREWS
INTO YOUR BRAIN
CAUSING YOUR PAIN
YOU SIT AND WATCH
HOLDING YOUR CROTCH
YOU'VE LOST YOUR POWER

CHEMTRAIL SHOWER
PINEAL GLAND
TURNED INTO SAND
AND AS YOU SLEEP
THEY KILL THE SHEEP
SO STOP THE TALK
AND LEARN TO WALK

TAXES

TAXES YOU MUST PAY
WARS EVERY DAY
YOU HAVE NO SAY
IT'S ALL THEIR WAY
SUCH SILENT SLAVES
DIGGING THEIR GRAVES
LIVING IN FEAR
LIKE HELPLESS DEER
ACTING SO BLIND
COURAGE CAN'T FIND
OH WHAT A SHAME
IT'S ALL THEIR GAME
NEW WARS EACH DAY
GUESS WHO DOES PAY

TEACHERS

THOSE TEACHERS
THOSE PREACHERS
WHO ARE THEY
EVERYDAY
TELLING YOU
WHAT TO DO
HOW TO LIVE
WHAT TO GIVE
CAN YOU LEARN
IT'S YOUR TURN
WHO YOU ARE

IT'S NOT FAR
NO TEACHERS
NO PREACHERS

TEARS

DO YOU HAVE TEARS
FOR EMPTY YEARS
OR ARE YOU FINE
SIPPING YOUR WINE
SO SEARCH YOUR SOUL
SET A NEW GOAL
THEN YOU WILL REACH
NATURE WILL TEACH
CLEAN OUT YOUR HEART
THE WAY TO START
EMPTY YOUR MIND
LOVE YOU WILL FIND
LOOK VERY DEEP
WALK FAST DON'T CREEP
FOR EMPTY YEARS
FREE ALL YOUR TEARS

TEARS (2)

TEARS IN MY HEART
WHEN DID IT START
A LONG TIME AGO
IT BEGAN TO SHOW
FULL OF SADNESS
LITTLE GLADNESS
EVEN AS A BOY
HARDLY ANY JOY
YET THROUGH IT ALL
I DID NOT FALL
I DREAMED OF HOPE
I LEARNED TO COPE
I CRIED I SWALLOWED TEARS

I OVERCAME MY FEARS
SOMEDAY IT WOULD BE TRUE
TO FIND MY LOVE IN YOU
MY SADNESS IS DONE
I HOPE TO HAVE FUN
AND THEN TEARS NO MORE
ENTERING LOVE'S DOOR
DREAMING OF THAT DAY
WHEN YOU COME MY WAY
TO STOP THE TEARS IN MY HEART
EACH OF US DOING OUR PART

THANK YOU

OH FATHER SKY
I WONDER WHY
EARTH MY MOTHER
SISTER BROTHER
YOU GIVE ME AIR
IT'S EVERYWHERE
YOU GIVE ME FOOD
YOU CHANGE MY MOOD
I SEE THE TREES
I FEEL THE BREEZE
LOOK AT THE BIRDS
AND THE COW TURDS
THE MONKEYS PLAY
OH WHAT A DAY
THE LIONS ROAR
THEY DON'T MAKE WAR
EAGLES SEE ALL
GIRAFFES STAND TALL
AND YOU ABOVE ALL
SO PLEASE DON'T STALL
THANK YOU I SAY
EVERY NEW DAY
OH FATHER SKY
I NOW KNOW WHY

THANK YOU GOD

THANK YOU GOD FOR BRINGING ME
 THROUGH THE DAY
THANK YOU GOD FOR SHOWING ME THE WAY
THANK YOU GOD FOR EVERYTHING YOU SAY
THANK YOU GOD FOR HELPING ME PRAY
I KNOW EVERYTHING THAT I MUST DO
ABLE TO START AND FOLLOW THROUGH
TO FOLLOW MY HEART AND BE TRUE
FREE LIKE A BIRD WHO FLEW AND FLEW
RIGHT THROUGH THE AIR
WITHOUT A CARE
NO MATTER WHERE
I WISH TO SHARE
THANK YOU ONCE AGAIN
FOR MOVING THIS PEN

THANK YOU GOD (2)

THANK YOU GOD FOR TODAY
TAKING MY PAIN AWAY
FOR MAKING ME NEVER FORGET
NEVER HAVING ANY REGRET
YOU BROUGHT ME COMFORT IN MY PAIN
MY BELIEF HAS NOT BEEN IN VAIN
WITH THESE WONDERFUL WORDS
I FLY FREE LIKE THE BIRDS
TO GO ANYWHERE I CHOOSE
KNOWING THAT I WILL NOT LOSE
I SAY ONCE AGAIN TO YOU
I KNOW MY LIFE IS NOT THROUGH

THANK YOU GOD (3)

THANK YOU GOD FOR THE DAY
THANK YOU FOR SHOWING ME THE WAY
THANK YOU LETTING ME PRAY

THANK YOU FOR WHAT YOU SAY
IVE LEARNED HOW TO BE
I'VE LEARNED HOW TO SEE
I'VE LEARNED TO RESPECT EVERY TREE
I'VE LEARNED TO RESPECT EVERY BEE
FOR ALL TOGETHER WE ARE WHOLE
FOR ALL TOGETHER WE ARE SOUL
FOR ALL TOGETHER WE REACH OUR GOAL
FOR ALL TOGETHER WE PLAY OUR ROLE
AND WITH ALL THIS IN MIND
AND WITH BEING VERY KIND
WE SHALL LEARN TO FIND
OUR PEACE OF MIND

THE BOSS

WE OWN YOUR MIND
TRUTH YOU CAN'T FIND
YOU ARE OUR SLAVE
FROM BIRTH TO GRAVE
WE MAKE THE WARS
WITHOUT A CAUSE
FOLLOW THE RULES
WE TEACH IN SCHOOLS
YOU HAVE NO CHOICE
YOU HAVE NO VOICE
YOU ARE NOT FREE
YOU CANNOT SEE
WAKE UP MY FRIEND
BEFORE THE END

THE CHILDREN

TEACH CHILDREN WHAT THEY NEED
TEACH THEM TO PLANT THE SEED
OF LOVE VALVES AND TRUTH
NOT TO BE SO UNCOUTH
KINDNESS AND HONESTY

THEN CLEARLY THEY WILL SEE
A BETTER WORLD TO LIVE
AND LEARNING HOW TO GIVE
MOTHER EARTH HER DUE
AND KEEP THE SKY BLUE
NO MORE ACID RAIN
NO MORE DEADLY PAIN
NO MORE LIVES IN VAIN
NO MORE WORLD INSANE
TEACH THEM HOW TO SAY
HARMONY AND SPIRIT
THEN MANKIND WILL HEAR IT
TEACH THEM WHAT THEY NEED
TEACH THEM TO PLANT THE SEED

THE DOLLAR

US DOLLAR
HEAR IT HOLLER
IT GETS SMALLER
PRICES TALLER
WHAT CAN WE DO
FOR ME AND YOU
GIVE SOLUTION
CONSTITUTION
WE NEED A JOB
HELP SAVE THE MOB
WE NEED TO LIVE
SO WHO WILL GIVE
THE THINGS WE NEED
GMO SEED
I DON'T THINK SO
NOT WAY TO GO
ANSWERS TO FIND
TO EASE MY MIND
HEAR IT HOLLAR
US DOLLAR

THE FOOL

TECHNOLOGY
PSYCHOLOGY
THEY OWN YOUR MIND
THEY KEEP YOU BLIND
YOU ARE ASLEEP
YOU DON'T MAKE A PEEP
SILENCE IS YOUR WAY
YOU PAY AND PAY
YOU BUY AND BUY
YOU NEVER SIGH
I WONDER WHY
YOU BUY THE LIE
BECAUSE YOU'RE STUCK
LIKE SITTING DUCK
YOUR MIND FROZEN
YOUR BRAIN DOZEN
NEVER TO WAKE
THEY EAT YOUR CAKE
PSYCHOLOGY
TECHNOLOGY

THE GAME

THE GAME OF LIFE
CHILDREN AND WIFE
CHASING MONEY
IS IT FUNNY
YOUR THOUGHTS CONTROLLED
ILLUSION MOLD
THINK YOU'RE SO SMART
HAVE A GOOD HEART
YOU TRY AND PLAN
COMPETE WITH MAN
YOU DO YOUR BEST
IN LIFE'S GREAT QUEST
THEN YOU AWAKE
MOUTH FULL OF CAKE

YOU SPIT IT OUT
GIVE A GREAT SHOUT
THEN YOU REALIZE
YOU WERE NOT WISE
YOU DID NOT KNOW
THE WAY TO GO
IT WAS A GAME
YOU HAD NO SHAME
THEY OWNED YOUR MIND
YOU TRIED TO FIND
YOUR WAY AROUND
THE EARTHLY GROUND
YOU HUGGED THE TREE
BEGAN TO SEE
THE IRONY
THEN YOU LOOKED UP
PUT DOWN YOUR CUP
YOU SAW THE SKY
STARTED TO CRY
HEARD NATURE'S SOUND
YOU FELT THE GROUND
AND ALL THE REST
YOU PASSED THE TEST
AND KISSED YOUR WIFE
NEW GAME OF LIFE

THE GOOD HEART

GOOD HEART IS SO BLIND
TO THE EVIL KIND
WILL IT THEN FIND
AN HONEST MIND?
THE GOOD HEART IS READY TO GIVE
TO HELP ANOTHER PERSON LIVE
WHEN WILL IT LEARN
TO HAVE IT'S TURN
TO BE ON THE RECEIVING END
NO LONGER HAVING TO DEFEND
GOOD HEART WANTS A CHANCE
TO ENJOY LIFE'S DANCE

WITHOUT HAVING TO WORRY
AND NOT HAVING TO HURRY
ON ITS WAY THROUGH LIFE
TO LIVE WITHOUT STRIFE
THE GOOD HEART IS SO BLIND
TO THE EVIL KIND
WHEN WILL IT FIND
AN HONEST MIND?

THE HEART'S NEW HOPE

THE HANGMAN'S ROPE
THE HEART'S NEW HOPE
THE BRAIN'S CONTROL
THE EGO'S ROLE
WORLD'S CONDITION
LACKS NUTRITION
AS YOU ALL SLEEP
ACTING LIKE SHEEP
THE HANGMAN COMES
INCREASES SLUMS
AND YOU COMPLAIN
BUT ALL IN VAIN
WAKE UP YOUR HEART
GET IT TO START
PUSH HANGMAN ASIDE
WHERE IS YOUR PRIDE
THE HEART'S NEW HOPE
CUT HANGMAN'S ROPE

THE MONEY GAME

THE MONEY GAME
IT HAS NO SHAME
WALL STREET BROKERS
BUNCH OF JOKERS
WILL SELL YOU ALL

UNTIL YOU FALL
SEE THE CARROT
JUST A PARROT
DOING ITS JOB
WORKING FOR MOB
WHITE COLLAR GUYS
ITS NO SURPRISE
OPEN YOUR EYES
AND BECOME WISE
IT HAS NO SHAME
THE MONEY GAME

THE MYSTIC

THINK YOU KNOW
HOW TO GROW
FOLLOW THE STAR
IT'S NOT FAR
UNKNOWN KIND
IN YOUR MIND
SEEING THE LIGHT
IN YOUR PLIGHT
ENERGY
SYNERGY
SPARKS THE WAY
A NEW DAY
THINK YOU KNOW
THEN YOU GROW

THE SLAVES

BANKS GUNS AND BOMBS
GMO FARMS
WE SIT LIKE FOOLS
WE ARE THEIR TOOLS
USED TIME AGAIN
TRAPPED IN A PEN
WE WAIT FOR CHANGE

IT'S OUT OF RANGE
IF WE JUST WAIT
THEN IT'S OUR FATE
SO WHAT WILL COME
HOPING THAT SOME
WILL STAND AND RISE
AND BECOME WISE
TRYING TO FIGHT
FOR WHAT IS RIGHT
WITH HELPLESS WORDS
LIKE DYING BIRDS
AGAINST THE POWER
BOMBS RAINING SHOWER
THE BANKS CONTROL
THEY OWN YOUR SOUL
BANKS GUNS AND BOMBS
GMO FARMS

THE SUN

UP COMES THE SUN
DAY HAS BEGUN
AND NOW THE FUN
LET'S WALK NOT RUN
THANKS FOR YOUR RAYS
THAT CREATE DAYS
ENERGY FINE
YOUR LOVE DIVINE
YOU GIVE US LIFE
WE MAKE OUR STRIFE
UNLESS WE KNOW
BEST WAY TO GO
SO HERE WE SEE
OUR LOVE FOR THEE
DAY HAS BEGUN
UP COMES THE SUN

THE TAO

FOLLOW THE TAO
I'LL SHOW YOU HOW
LEARN NATURE'S WAY
LIVE THEM ALL DAYS
AND SO FIND PEACE
AND JOY INCREASE
AND WHEN YOU DO
YOU WILL FIND YOU
AND THEN YOU KNOW
WHERE LIFE WILL GO
NOTHING TO SEEK
END OF THE WEEK
YOU ARE THERE NOW
TO NATURE BOW
I'LL SHOW YOU HOW
FOLLOW THE TAO

THE TIME IS HERE

THE TIME IS HERE
LOSE ALL YOUR FEAR
TAKE ACTIONS BRAVE
BE NOT A SLAVE
SO DON'T DELAY
BE ON YOU WAY
AND HAVE YOUR SAY
THIS IS YOUR DAY
NO TIME TO LOSE
WILL NOT EXCUSE
YOU MUST ACT
IT'S A FACT
FOR IF YOU WAIT
YOU'LL HAVE NO PLATE
LOSE ALL YOU FEAR
YOUR TIME IS HERE

THE WORST KILLER

THE WORST KILLER
MURDERER THRILLER
KILLS ANIMAL
WAS CANNIBAL
KILLS ALL THE FISH
MAKES TASTY DISH
KILLS MANY BIRDS
KILLS MANY HERDS
CUTS DOWN THE TREES
POISONS THE BEES
POLLUTES WATER
RAPES HIS DAUGHTER
POLLUTES THE AIR
DRONES EVERYWHERE
SOIL IS DESTROYED
DOLLAR MADE VOID
HUMANITY
INSANITY
STOP THIS KILLER
INSANE THRILLER
OR YOU WILL DIE
AND WONDER WHY
SO WAKE UP NOW
USE THE OLD PLOW
AND PLANT THE SEED
QUICKLY TAKE HEED
HURRY IT'S LATE
AND CLEAN THE SLATE
TAKE BACK CONTROL
IT IS YOUR ROLE
STOP THE KILLER
END THE THRILLER

THINK ABOUT IT

NOTHING IS YOURS
IT'S A FALSE CAUSE

YOU'RE MADE TO THINK
YOU OWN THE SINK
YOUR HOUSE YOUR CAR
THE COOKIE JAR
THE MONEY MADE
THE MONEY PAID
YOUR DOG AND CAT
THE BASEBALL BAT
EVEN YOUR CHILD
AND NATURE'S WILD
IT DISAPPEARS
WHEN YOU LOSE FEARS
YOUR BODY TOO
IT IS NOT YOU
YOU ARE SPIRIT
IF YOU HEAR IT
A SPECK OF LIGHT
IN DAY OR NIGHT
THINKING YOU OWN
YOUR NEW CELL PHONE
THIS IS MY LAND
LINE IN THE SAND
YOU WORK FOR MORE
YOU STORE AND STORE
THEN YOU REALIZE
YOU BECOME WISE
IT'S A FALSE CAUSE
NOTHING IS YOURS

THINK ABOUT IT (2)

IF YOU THINK ABOUT IT
YOU'LL BEGIN TO TAUT IT
SOCIETY GETS WORSE
IT'S MANKIND'S NEW CURSE
DESTROYING OURSELVES
NO MORE LITTLE ELVES
AS POLLUTION INCREASES
NATURAL LIVING CEASES
THE AIR GOES BAD

OH IT'S SO SAD
THE SOIL IS DEPLETED
WE ARE ALL VERY CHEATED
PESTICIDES AND SPRAYS
WILL SHORTEN OUR DAYS
CREATING MORE DRUGS
KILLING ALL THE BUGS
BUT NEW ONES GROW
THEY WIN THE SHOW
RIVERS ARE UNCLEAN
GARBAGE DUMPS ARE SEEN
MORE MONEY FOR THE RICH
ISN'T IT TIME TO SWITCH
FROM THOSE WHO CONTROL
WE ALL PAY THE TOLL
WITH MORE DISEASE
LOSING THE TREES
PAYING TRILLIONS
KILLING MILLIONS
PRETENDING NOT TO KNOW
THE RIGHT WAY WE MUST GO
STOP THE GREED
PLANT THE SEED
WE MUST LIVE TOGETHER
LIKE BIRDS OF A FEATURE
IF NOT OUR CHILDREN WILL DIE
WE ALL KNOW THE REASON WHY
UNLESS WE STOP NOW
AND TO NATURE BOW
THE EARTH WILL BEGIN TO END
THE CORPORATIONS MUST BEND
WE MUST CHANGE OUR WAYS
AND CREATE GOOD DAYS
IF YOU THINK ABOUT IT
YOU'LL BEGIN TO TAUT IT

THINK CLEARLY

THINK CLEARLY
LOVE DEARLY

GIVE YOUR ALL
DOWN THE WALL
WHEN YOU DO
YOU'LL FEEL NEW
CLOSER TO BE
THEN TO SEE
A NEW WAY
LIVE THE DAY
SO TO FIND
LOVING MIND
LOVE DEARLY
THINK CLEARLY

THOUSAND WORDS

THOUSAND WORDS
FLOCK OF BIRDS
THROUGH THE AIR
EVERYWHERE
EARS AND EYES
CHILDREN'S CRIES
MOTHER'S SIGHS
HUMAN LIES
OVER AND DONE
LIFE'S BEGUN
BETTER DAYS
WITH NEW WAYS
FLOCK OF BIRDS
THOUSAND WORDS

TIME HAS COME

THE TIME HAS COME
THAT EVEN SOME
HAVE LOST THEIR FEAR
HOLD FREEDOM DEAR
LIFT THEIR HEADS HIGH
AND SEE THE SKY

DON'T WONDER WHY
THEY KNOW THE LIE
READY TO DO
WITH HEARTS SO TRUE
WHATEVER IT TAKES
GOODBYE TO FAKES
COURAGE AND BRAVE
NO LONGER SLAVE
THE TIME HAS COME
FOR MORE THAN SOME

TIME PASSES

WHO IS THAT I SEE LOOKING THAT WAY
I NEVER USED TO BE OLD AND GREY
I USED TO BE YOUNG AND GAY
I THOUGHT I'D ALWAYS STAY THAT WAY
BUT NOW I KNOW I TOO MUST GO
JUST LIKE THE REST
I'D DO MY BEST
ON EVERY TEST
AND TRY AS I MAY
WITH EVERY PASSING DAY
I TOO BECAME OLD AND GREY
BUT I REALIZED NOW
AND LEARNED HOW
TO LIVE A BETTER LIFE
AND REDUCE MY STRIFE
SINCE I LEARNED WHAT TO DO
WAS TO KEEP LOVING YOU!

TO DR INA

YOU ARE FORTY TWO
YOU KNOW JUST WHAT TO DO
IF YOU STOP AND THINK
YOU'LL STAY IN THE PINK
KEEP YOU BODY CLEAN

BE HAPPY NOT MEAN
IN MORNING WHEN YOU AWAKE
A GOOD BREAKFAST YOU WILL TAKE
MAKE SURE YOU HAVE A GOOD LUNCH
SPINACH, CARROTS BY THE BUNCH
DINNER WILL BE HEALTHY TOO
YOU KNOW WHAT YOU NEED TO DO
BE SURE TO SLEEP EIGHT HOURS
AND TAKE ENOUGH GOOD SHOWERS
WHEN ALL IS SAID AND DONE
KEEP ON HAVING YOUR FUN
I KNOW ITS NOT SO NICE
TO GIVE YOU MY ADVICE
SO I WILL STOP HERE
HAPPY BIRTHDAY DEAR

TRUTH

FACING THE TRUTH
OLD AGE OR YOUTH
IT'S HERE TO STAY
WON'T GO AWAY
AND LEARN IT NOW
TO NATURE BOW
ANIMALS TREES
FLOWERS AND LEAVES
SEE THE SUN SET
WITHOUT REGRET
MOON AND THE STARS
PLUTO AND MARS
GREEDY PEOPLE
THE CHURCH STEEPLE
PEOPLE OF LOVE
THE SKY ABOVE
SOME KILL THE COWS
SOME LOVING BOWS
DO WHAT YOU CHOOSE
NATURE WON'T LOSE
FACING THE TRUTH
OLD AGE OR YOUTH

TRUTH (2)

SEARCHING FOR TRUTH
YOU LOST YOUR YOUTH
THERE'S NO SUCH THING
ONLY LIFE'S STING
WHICH WAKES YOU UP
LIKE COFFEE CUP
AND WHEN AWAKE
YOU START TO SHAKE
BECAUSE YOU FIND
A LOVELY MIND
THAT GUIDES YOU THROUGH
TO INSIDE YOU
AND THERE YOU ARE
NOT VERY FAR
FROM YOUR OWN TRUTH
REGAIN YOUR YOUTH

UNDERSTAND

UNDERSTAND LIFE
LIVE WITHOUT STRIFE
OPEN YOUR MIND
THERE YOU WILL FIND
CAPACITY
VORACITY
THEN YOU WILL KNOW
LIFE'S JUST A SHOW
WHEREVER YOU GO
WHERE WINDS DO BLOW
WITH EBB AND FLOW
ABOVE BELOW
EARTH MOON AND STARS
JUNIPER MARS
AND ALL AROUND
YOU HEAR THE SOUND
THE PULSE AND HEART
THE BRAND NEW START
FOLLOW THIS RHYME
AND TAKE YOUR TIME
GET A FRONT SEAT
ENJOY THE TREAT
LIFE'S JUST A SHOW
YOU COME AND GO

USELESS WORDS

SOME USELESS WORDS
FLY LIKE THE BIRDS
THEY GO NOWHERE
JUST HERE AND THERE
IDEAS THAT LIVE
WATER IN SIEVE
IF NOTHING'S DONE
THEN NOTHING WON
EVOLUTION
REVOLUTION
STAY CALM AND WAIT
LIKE A NEW DATE
THEN YOU WILL SEE
WHAT IS TO BE
FLY LIKE THE BIRDS
SOME USELESS WORDS

VACCINATION

VACCINATION
FOR THE NATION
EBOLA HERE
AND NOW YOU FEAR
DO WHAT YOU'RE TOLD
DO NOT BE BOLD
OR OFF YOU GO
TO FEMA SHOW
AND THERE YOU'LL FIND
NO PEACE OF MIND
YOU MUST OBEY
DO WHAT THEY SAY
MEDIA KNOWS
PUTS ON GOOD SHOWS
SO UNDERSTAND
ON YOUR FEET LAND
AND LEARN THE GAME
AND HAVE NO SHAME
YOU NEED TO KNOW
WHICH WAY TO GO
AND GET THERE FAST
SO YOU CAN LAST
HURRY HURRY
AND DON'T WORRY
THERE'S STILL SOME TIME
REREAD THIS RHYME

VISION CLEAR

VISION CLEAR
YOU ARE NEAR
LOVE IS HERE
HERE YOU STAY
ALL THE DAY
IT'S OUR WAY
TO FIND JOY
IN LOVE'S TOY
PEACE OF MIND
WE CAN FIND
BEING KIND
LOVE IS HERE
VISION CLEAR

WILL BE YOUR FATE
SIT AND BE STILL
YOUR MIND WILL FILL
TIME FOR A SONG
WAITING SO LONG

WAIT FOR GOD

IF WE DON'T KNOW HOW TO WAIT
WE WILL NEVER BECOME GREAT
WHEN WE KNOW WHICH WAY TO TURN
THEN WE WILL BEGIN TO LEARN
GOD HAS THE WAYS
DURING YOUR DAYS
AS EACH ONE PASSES
WALKING ON GRASSES
CLOSE TO NATURE ALL THE TIME
SINGING AND MAKING A RHYME
AND WHEN THE TIME IS RIGHT
YOU AND GOD BEING TIGHT
YOU'LL ALWAYS FIND YOUR WAY
HAVE A WONDERFUL DAY
GOD WILL ALWAYS COME
TO THOSE SPECIAL SOME
WHO HAVE LEARNED TO WAIT
TO BECOME SO GREAT.

WAITING

WAITING SO LONG
TIME FOR A SONG
TO CALM MY MIND
THUS PEACE TO FIND
AND SO I LEARN
TO WAIT MY TURN
IT COMES IN TIME
WITH THIS NEW RHYME
AND MAYBE YOU
WILL LEARN THIS TOO
SOMETIMES TO WAIT

WAKING UP

LAND OF THE FREE
WHY CAN'T YOU SEE
HOME OF THE BRAVE
YOU ARE A SLAVE
THE TIME HAS COME
FOR ONLY SOME
TO UNDERSTAND
THIS IS YOUR LAND
SO LEARN TO DO
RED WHITE AND BLUE
GOOD LOOK AROUND
TILL PEACE IS FOUND
AS YOU AWAKE
FOR CHILDREN'S SAKE
SEE ALL THE LIES
WAKE UP GET WISE
THE TIME IS NEAR
YOUR LIFE IS DEAR
YOU CANNOT WAIT
IT'S VERY LATE
YOU SIT AND THINK
DEEPER YOU SINK
SO CHANGE YOUR MIND
SOLUTION FIND
IT'S UP TO YOU
FIND WHAT TO DO
LAND OF THE FREE
FOR YOU AND ME

WAR

MAKE WAR
NO MORE
THEY SAID
NO DEAD
MUST STOP
KILLED POP
MOTHER
BROTHER
PEACE RISE
NO LIES
LOVE COMES
NO BUMS
NO MORE
MAKE WAR

WAR FOR MONEY

KILL FOR MONEY
NO BEES NO HONEY
THE WAR MACHINE
DESTROYS THE GREEN
YOU SIT AND WAIT
IT'S NOT YOUR FATE
SO FIGHT FOR PEACE
AND NEVER CEASE
OPEN YOUR MIND
THERE YOU WILL FIND
THE WAY TO GO
THEN YOU WILL KNOW
FOR IF YOU DON'T
AND SAY YOU WON'T
YOUR CHILDREN DIE
AND AS YOU SIGH
AND WAKE UP LATE
TO CHANGE THEIR FATE
SO START TO THINK
BEFORE YOU SINK

WAR FOR MONEY
IS NOT FUNNY

WAR NO MORE

WAR NO MORE
CLOSE THE DOOR
VIOLENCE
SILENCE
PLEASE AWAKE
FOR YOUR SAKE
TAKE A STAND
IT'S YOUR LAND
IT'S YOUR LIFE
HUSBAND WIFE
CHILDREN TOO
EVEN YOU
CLOSE THE DOOR
WAR NO MORE

WAR WAR WAR

WAR WAR WAR
CLOSE THE DOOR
WASTE WASTE WASTE
ACT IN HASTE
STOP IT NOW
WE KNOW HOW
IN MAN'S MIND
THERE YOU FIND
FEAR AND GREED
SO TAKE HEED
PLANT THE SEED
RID THE WEED
CLOSE THE DOOR
WAR NO MORE

WATCH THE BALLOON

WATCH THE BALLOON
LOOK AT THE MOON
SEE ILLUSIONS
THINK CONFUSIONS
WE OWN YOUR MIND
YOU CANNOT FIND
ACTION TO TAKE
FOR YOUR OWN SAKE
YOU HAVE YOUR FOOD
KEEPS YOUR GOOD MOOD
WHAT A LONG SLEEP
A BILLION SHEEP
AS BOMBS EXPLODE
SO CLOSE THE ROAD
TAKE ANOTHER PILL
TO KEEP YOU STILL
YOU'RE PROTECTED
RESURRECTED
AND WHEN YOU DIE
WITH YOUR LAST SIGH
AND YOUR LAST WORD
THEN WILL BE HEARD
WATCH THE BALLOON
IT WILL BURST SOON

WATCHING

MANY TRILLIONS
PAYMENTS MILLIONS
WATCHING IT GO
NOTHING TO KNOW
JUST SIT AND READ
EMPTY MINDS FEED
HELPLESS WE THINK
ECONOMY SINK
FEARFUL FACES
ALL THE RACES

JUST SOME MORE TALK
NEVER THE WALK
SO WHEN AND WHERE
GIVE UP THE STARE
PAYMENTS MILLIONS
BORROW TRILLIONS

WATCHING (2)

WATCHING THE WORLD GO BY
IN SILENCE I DO CRY
I ALWAYS WONDER WHY
SO I LOOK TO THE SKY
AND THERE IS WHERE I SEE
A LITTLE HOPE FOR ME
ITS ALWAYS NICE AND BLUE
CLOUDS AND RAIN AND SUN TOO
IT'S NOT THAT I AM SAD
OR EVEN VERY GLAD
I WATCH DAYS AS THEY PASS
SITTING ON THE NICE GRASS
AND IN MY HEART I KNOW
I'LL HAVE SOMEWHERE TO GO
FIND MY BEAUTIFUL DREAM
HOPING THE WORLD WOULD SEEM
TO BE A LOVING PLACE
NOT A HUMAN DISGRACE
AND SO WITH THESE LAST WORDS
I LIFT EYES TO THE BIRDS
AS THEY FLY ABOVE ME
I KNOW THEY ALL LOVE ME

WATCHING (3)

ARE YOU WATCHING THE MOVIES OR THE
    NEWS
IT'S UP TO YOU TO CHOOSE
BOTH SEEM TO BE THE SAME

VIOLENCE, GREED AND SHAME
FANTASY AND REALITY COINCIDE
BE IT KILLING, BOMBING OR TAKING A BRIDE
YOU NO LONGER KNOW WHAT IS REAL
THE CAMERA WILL ALWAYS CONCEAL
IS IT TRUTH OR A LIE
IT MAKES ME WONDER WHY
THE WORLD HAS GONE CRAZY
CHECKING ON MISS DAISY
IF YOU WONDER WHICH CHANNEL TO CHECK
DOUBLE CLICK AND REARRANGE YOUR NECK
IT DOESN'T MATTER WHAT YOU DO
IT IS NO LONGER UP TO YOU
YOU'RE JUST AN OBSERVER
SEARCHING FOR LOVE
AND THE SKY ABOVE
THEN ARE YOU CONFUSED
WHICH CHANNEL YOU CHOOSE

WATER

WATER HERE
WATER DEAR
WATER NEAR
WATER CLEAR
WE NEED YOU
AND AIR TOO
FOOD ALIVE
WE CAN THRIVE
ALL OF THESE
IF YOU PLEASE
KEEP US GOING
EARTH'S LOVE SHOWING
WATER DEAR
WATER CLEAR

WE ARE

WE ARE THE SUN
WE ARE THE STARS
WE ARE THE SEAS
WE ARE THE LAND
WE ARE THE TREES
WE ARE THE ANIMALS
WE ARE THE BIRDS
WE ARE THE INSECTS
WE ARE THE PLANTS
WE ARE THE SPIRITS
WE ARE THE PEOPLE
WE ARE THE LOVE
WE ARE THE GODS
WE ARE EVERYTHING
WE ARE THE HEARTS
WE ARE NATURE
WE ARE ONE
SO WHO ARE YOU?

WE ARE ALL ONE

WE ARE ALL ONE
LOVE NOT A GUN
WORK TOGETHER
THE SAME FEATHER
SO UNDERSTAND
LIFE CAN BE GRAND
BUT IF YOU SLEEP
AND ACT LIKE SHEEP
THE PLANET DIES
DUE TO BIG LIES
THE TIME IS SHORT
LIFE MAY ABORT
DEPENDS ON YOU
AND WHAT YOU DO
AND HOW YOU THINK
STAND ALIVE DON'T SINK

AND WAIT NO MORE
OPEN THE DOOR
LET LOVE COME IN
BANISH THE SIN
LOVE NOT A GUN
WE ARE ALL ONE

WHEN WE SAT BY THE FIRE
VOWED NOT TO BE A LIAR
AND NOW YEARS HAVE PASSED AWAY
REMEMBER WHAT I SAY
OH, WHAT A GREAT DAY
TO BE ON MY WAY

WE ARE NOT SLAVES

WE ARE NOT SLAVES
WE ARE NOT KNAVES
WE SEE THE LIGHT
NO NEED TO FIGHT
THE WAY IS CLEAR
WE HAVE NO FEAR
EVERY NEW DAY
WE CLEAR THE WAY
AS TRUTH UNFOLD
OUR STORY IS TOLD
AS THE WORLD SEES
WE'RE OFF OUR KNEES
WE ARE NOT KNAVES
AND NOT YOUR SLAVES

WHAT A DAY

WHAT A DAY
ON MY WAY
SO MANY THINGS TO DO
WISH I WAS HERE WITH YOU
YOU ARE SO FAR
ACROSS THE BAR
BUT I THINK OF YOU
MY LOVE IS SO TRUE
AS I DO MY CHORES
AND CLEANING MY DRAWERS
I REMEMBER
THAT COLD DECEMBER

WHAT DOES GOD SAY?

TELL ME WHAT DOES GOD SAY
I LISTEN EVERY DAY
GOD TELLS ME WHAT TO DO
SENDS A MESSAGE TO YOU
OPEN YOUR HEART
GET A FRESH START
YESTERDAY IS DONE
TODAY WILL BE WON
GET READY TO HEAR
LET GO OF YOUR FEAR
READY TO BEGIN
THERE'LL BE NO MORE SIN
EVERYTHING WILL FALL IN PLACE
A CHANCE FOR THE HUMAN RACE
TO CLEAN ALL THE POLLUTION
THERE IS NO SUBSTITUTION
WHEN ALL THIS IS DONE
CHILDREN WILL HAVE FUN
AND NOT DIE OF CANCER
GOD'S VOICE IS THE ANSWER.

WHAT DO YOU SEE

WHAT DO YOU SEE
HOW SHOULD YOU BE
CHOICES YOU MAKE
EACH BREATH YOU TAKE
HEARING THE SOUND

FEET ON THE GROUND
HEAD UP SO HIGH
WONDERING WHY
YOU CANNOT FIND
YOUR GOOD OLD MIND
OH WHAT TO DO
THE LIFE OF YOU
AND THERE YOU ARE
TOUCHING THE STAR
HOW SHOULD YOU BE
WHAT DO YOU SEE

WHAT IF

IF YOU COULD SEE
YOU ARE NOT FREE
YOUR ARE AWAKE
A GOOD LOOK TAKE
DO WHAT YOU'RE TOLD
AS YOU GROW OLD
OBEY CONFORM
FOLLOW THE NORM
YOUR CHILD YOU TEACH
OH HOW YOU PREACH
THE THINGS TO BUY
AND WHEN TO CRY
AND WHAT TO SAY
DURING THE DAY
WHAT IF YOU CHANGE
GO OUT OF RANGE
OF LOVE YOU TALK
AND WALK THE WALK
IF YOU COULD SEE
HELP THEM BE FREE

WHAT IS THE GAME

WHAT IS THE GAME
PLAYED WITHOUT SHAME
CORPORATIONS
CONTROL NATIONS
CONTROL YOUR MIND
MONEY TO FIND
ALL FROM YOUR SWEAT
WITHOUT REGRET
YOU'RE JUST A SLAVE
A ZOMBIE KNAVE
SO WAKE UP NOW
PUT DOWN THEIR PLOW
DO YOUR OWN THING
FLY ON YOUR WING
USE YOUR MIND
BE LOVING KIND
FOR IN YOUR HEART
THE PLACE TO START
WHAT IS THEIR GAME
PLAYED WITHOUT SHAME

WHAT TO DO

WHAT SHOULD I DO
I'M ASKING YOU
CAUSE I DON'T KNOW
WHICH WAY TO GO
I'VE TRIED ALL THE WAYS
DURING ALL MY DAYS
AND NOW I SEE
DEEP INTO ME
NEW THINGS FOR ME TO LEARN
A RIGHT OR A LEFT TURN
THAT'S WHY I ASK
WHAT IS MY TASK
WHAT'S PAST IS DONE
THE BATTLE WON

WHAT LIES AHEAD
CANNOT BE READ
IN ANY BOOK
SO I MUST LOOK
AND ASK YOU
WHAT TO DO

WHAT'S HAPPENING?

WHAT HAS COME TO PASS?
MORE CEMENT AND LESS GRASS
FEWER TREES
GOD, PLEASE
OPEN THEIR EYES
AND STOP THE LIES
THE FASTER WE GO
THE GREATER THE SHOW
AT LEAST SO WE THINK
WE ARE ON THE BRINK
WHERE IS MAN GOING?
LOVE IS NOT SHOWING
AS THE EARTH GETS WORSE
IT'S MANKIND'S NEW CURSE
CREATING SUCH DISASTER
EVERYTHING GOING FASTER
SO HERE WE ARE
NOT VERY FAR
FROM FACING OUR DEEDS
SUPERSONIC SPEEDS
THE EARTH IS NOT PURE
OF THAT I AM SURE
SO LET'S DO OUR BEST
IT'S THE FINAL TEST

WHAT'S NEW

SO WHAT'S NEW
INSIDE YOU
IT'S BEEN THERE
NOW AWARE
YOU HAVE FOUND
SOME OLD GROUND
NOW YOU KNOW
THE OLD SHOW
THIS IN MIND
YOU NOW FIND
A NEW LIFE
WITHOUT STRIFE
INSIDE YOU
SO WHAT'S NEW

WHAT'S NEW (2)

WITH EACH DAY'S NEWS
THEY TURN THE SCREWS
CONTROL YOUR MIND
TRUTH NEVER FIND
KEEP YOU SPINNING
WHO KEEPS WINNING
SO BREAK AWAY
CREATE YOUR DAY
LEARN THE GAME
PLAY WITHOUT SHAME
TAKE CHARGE OF LIFE
REMOVE THE KNIFE
WORRY NO MORE
OPEN THE DOOR
TO FIND YOUR PEACE
LOVE NEVER CEASE
YOU'RE IN CONTROL
IT'S YOUR NEW ROLE
NO MORE FAKE NEWS
AND NO MORE BLUES

WHEN TWO HEARTS BECOME ONE

WHEN TWO HEARTS BECOME ONE
YOU WILL HAVE SO MUCH FUN
YOUR HEART JUST MELTS AWAY
THERE YOU WILL WANT TO STAY
YOU WILL FEEL SUCH GOOD JOY
LIKE A GIRL AND A BOY
YOU FORGET THE WHOLE WORLD
CAUSE YOUR LOVE IS UNFURLED
YOU LONG FOR THE FEELING
YOUR LOVE IS REVEALING
WHEN TWO HEARTS BECOME ONE
LIFE TURNS FROM PAIN TO FUN

WHERE ARE YOU

WHERE ARE YOU
IS IT TRUE
THAT YOU'RE HERE
EVER NEAR
OH HOW NICE
LOVE'S GOOD SPICE
OH SUCH JOY
GIRL AND BOY
PLAYING GAMES
WITHOUT NAMES
SOMETHING NEW
THEY CAN DO
IS IT TRUE
WHERE ARE YOU

WHEN YOUR HEART SLEEPS

WHEN YOUR HEART SLEEPS
THE WORLD HEART WEEPS
MISSES YOUR LOVE
GIVE IT A SHOVE
WAKE IT UP NOW
LOVE TAKE A BOW
AND JOIN US ALL
LOVE STAND UP TALL
FEEL YOUR HEART FILL
ENJOY THE THRILL
AWAKENED HEART
THE PLACE TO START
WHEN YOUR HEART SLEEPS
THE WORLD HEAT WEEPS

WHERE ARE YOU GOING?

WHERE ARE YOUR GOING
WITHOUT YOU KNOWING?
YOU TRAVEL SO FAST
WILL YOU EVER LAST?
FROM POINT A TO B
NOTHING DO YOU SEE
FROM POINT C TO D
LITTLE LEFT OF THEE
THEN FASTER YOU GO
SURELY YOU DON'T KNOW
AS YOU TRAVEL ON YOUR WAY
DOING THE SAME THING EACH DAY
IF YOU COULD STOP A BIT
AND IN YOUR GOOD CHAIR SIT
AND BECOME AWARE
IF ONLY YOU DARE

TO THINK SOME MORE
AND FIND THE DOOR
WHERE ARE YOU GOING
WITHOUT YOU KNOWING?

WHERE IS GOD

WHERE IS GOD I ASK EVERY NIGHT
I TUCK MYSELF INTO BED TIGHT
I WANT TO DO EVERYTHING RIGHT
SO I SPEAK TO GOD EVERY NIGHT
I WAIT FOR ANSWERS TO MY PRAYERS
HOPING I WILL GET ALL MY SHARES
SO I CONCENTRATE VERY HARD
AND SO I LET GO OF MY GUARD
IT'S THE ONLY WAY TO RECEIVE
VERY LONG AWAITED REPRIEVE
SO THAT I WILL SUFFER NO MORE
FINALLY TO REACH THE NEW SHORE
SOON I WILL CLOSE MY EYES
TO FIND A GOOD SURPRISE
AS I DREAM OF MY GOD
IT'S REALLY NOT SO HARD!

WHERE TO GO

WHERE TO GO
I DON'T KNOW
TRAVEL FAR
TO A STAR
NORTH EAST WEST
WHICH IS BEST
SOUTH I GO
THERE'S NO SNOW
WATER'S WARM
SUMMER STORM
SUNNY DAYS
LOVELY HAZE

I DON'T KNOW
WHERE TO GO

WHERE TO GO (2)

WHERE TO GO
I DON'T KNOW
I'VE BEEN HERE BEEN THERE
I'VE BEEN EVERYWHERE
TRIED THE BIG CITY
IT WAS SO PRETTY
TRIED THE COUNTRYSIDE
MOUNTAINS PLAINS SO WIDE
BEEN IN BARS
WENT TO MARS
VERY LONG TRIPS
ON BIG SHIPS
LOOKING FOR HOME
READ EVERY POEM
SEARCHING TO FIND
SOME PEACE OF MIND
AND FINALLY FOUND
THIS BEAUTIFUL GROUND
HERE UNDER MY FEET
IT WAS ALL SO NEAT
NOT WANTING TO GO
BECAUSE NOW I KNOW
THE ANSWER IS HERE
NEXT TO YOU MY DEAR

WHERE TO GO (3)

AS I WAIT TO FIND MY WAY
LOOKING FOR A BETTER DAY
I THINK WHAT TO SAY
AND BEGIN TO PRAY
TO RELIEVE THE PAIN
TO LIVE WITHOUT STRAIN

TO GO ON WITH MY LIFE
LIVING IT WITHOUT STRIFE
GOODBYE TO THE PAST
IT ALL WENT SO FAST
IT'S OVERT AND DONE
SADNESS AND THE FUN
LIVING HERE AND NOW
FIND MY WAY SOMEHOW
FOR A BRIGHT NEW DAY
ALL GOOD THINGS TO SAY
LOOKING AT THE SKY
AND WONDERING WHY
TOOK SO LONG TO KNOW
THE RIGHT WAY TO GO

WHITE CLOUD

GREAT WHITE CLOUD
SPEAK SO LOUD
THUNDERS VOICE
SO REJOICE
RAIN DOES FALL
GRASS GROWS TALL
RIVERS GROW
SEEDS TO SOW
FOOD TO EAT
WHAT A TREAT
OH HOW NEAT
GREAT RED BEET
SPEAK SO LOUD
RAINING CLOUD

WHO AM I

I KEEP SEARCHING
MIND IS LURCHING
SEARCH HERE AND THERE
LOOKED EVERYWHERE
TRIED EVERYTHING
FLEW ON BIRD'S WING
WENT ON A HORSE
I ASKED MY BOSS
I ASKED MY WIFE
TO END MY STRIFE
SHE DID NOT KNOW
WHERE I SHOULD GO
WENT TO CHURCH
LEFT IN A LURCH
MY FRIEND SAID LOOK
OPEN GOOD BOOK
MIRROR I TRIED
EYES OPEN WIDE
I SAW MY FACE
HASTENED MY PACE
I TRIED IT ALL
HIT HEAD ON WALL
I HEARD A VOICE
IT SAID REJOICE
NOW LOOK INSIDE
AND LOSE MY PRIDE
AND BE HUMBLE
I WON'T STUMBLE
AND FEEL MY PEACE
LOVE NEVER CEASE
AND SEE MY HEART
HURRY AND START
WHO WILL I BE
WHEN I CAN SEE
I SEARCHED AND FOUND
MY INNER GROUND
NOW I CAN SEE
I AM JUST ME

WHO AM I (2)

TELL ME WHO AM I
AND THEN TELL ME WHY
DID I GET THIS WAY

154

WITH SO MUCH TO SAY
I AM SO CONFUSED
AM I OVER USED
I HAVE NO IDEA
I LIVE WITHOUT FEAR
DON'T KNOW WHAT I DO
ALWAYS LOVING YOU
I WILL SOON FIND OUT
WHAT IT'S ALL ABOUT
AS I SEARCH MY MIND
AND THERE I WILL FIND
I AM JUST A MAN
DOING WHAT I CAN

WHO ARE YOU?

WHO ARE YOU?
TO TREAT ME LIKE THIS
YOU EAT MY FRUIT
YOU BREATHE MY OXYGEN
YOU PRUNE MY BRANCHES
YOUR DOG PISSES ON ME
YOU PUT SOME NAILS IN ME
YOU HANG SIGNS ON ME
YOU PUT CHEMICALS ON ME
YOU BURN MY FALLEN LEAVES
WHEN I DON'T PRODUCE ENOUGH
YOU CUT ME DOWN
YOU DIG OUT MY ROOTS
YOU DESTROY MY BIRD'S HOME
YOUR BURN MY LIMBS
YOU DROWN MY ASHES
WHY DON'T YOU LET ME DIE IN PEACE?
YOU DON'T RESPECT ME
WHO ARE YOU?
TO TREAT ME LIKE THIS
I'M ALIVE
I HAVE FEELINGS
DO YOU THINK YOU ARE BETTER THAN ME?
IT'S TIME YOU WOKE UP

IF YOU DON'T
YOU'LL DIE

WHO ARE YOU? (2)

ALWAYS CHASING
ALWAYS RACING
ALWAYS GOING
WITHOUT KNOWING
GET IT DONE FAST
THE TASKS ARE VAST
SO MAKE A LIST
YOUR ARM YOU TWIST
YOU CANNOT WAIT
YOU MUST BE GREAT
YOU MAKE YOUR PLANS
YOU USE YOUR HANDS
YOU USE YOUR HEAD
SOME TEARS YOU SHED
THEN YOU AWAKE
YOUR HEAD YOU SHAKE
YOU HEAR THE PHONE
AND THEN YOU GROAN
ALWAYS RACING
ALWAYS CHASING

WHY DO I CRY?

WHY DO I CRY?
I WONDER WHY
I CRY SO MUCH
CAUSE I'M IN TOUCH
WITH ALL MY SADNESS AND PAIN
LIFE THAT I'LL NEVER REGAIN
THE TEARS ROLL DOWN MY FACE
HOPING TO FIND MY PLACE
IN A HAPPIER LIFE
LESS EMOTIONAL STRIFE

FILLED WITH LOVE
FROM ABOVE
UNLESS I CAN FIND
SOMEONE WHO IS KIND
HERE ON EARTH TODAY
FINDING A NEW WAY
SO I DON'T CRY ANYMORE
WHEN I OPEN LOVE'S NEW DOOR
WHY DO I CRY?
NOW I KNOW WHY

IT'S NATURE'S LAW
THAT EAGLES SOAR
SO VERY HIGH
IN THE BLUE SKY
CLOUDS ARE SO WHITE
NEVER GET UP TIGHT
DOING ALL RIGHT
SEEING THE LIGHT
WITH SPIRITS HIGH
NOW I KNOW WHY
LIKE A FINE LACE
WIND IN MY FACE

WILL YOU REVEAL

WILL YOU REVEAL
ALL THAT YOU FEEL
OR WILL YOU HIDE
BEHIND YOUR PRIDE
BETTER TO LOVE
WITH LIGHT ABOVE
SEE THE BRIGHT STAR
FROM WHERE YOU ARE
FLY TO THE MOON
I'LL SEE YOU SOON
THERE YOU WILL FIND
SOME PEACE OF MIND
NO WARS NO FIGHTS
GOOD HUMAN RIGHTS
MANY NEW STARTS
NEW RACE OF HEARTS
WILL YOU REVEAL
ALL THAT YOU FEEL

WISDOM

WISDOM NEEDED
WISE WORDS HEEDED
WHERE ARE THEY FOUND
ON NATURE'S GROUND
GRASS FLOWERS PLANTS
LEARN FROM THE ANTS
WORK TOGETHER
BIRDS OF A FEATHER
FLYING SO HIGH
IN THE BLUE SKY
LANDING ON TREES
PEOPLE THEY PLEASE
COLORS SO FINE
LIKE A GOOD WINE
TASTES TO ENJOY
THAT'S NATURES PLOY
WISE WORDS NEEDED
WISDOM HEEDED

WIND

WIND IN MY FACE
LIKE A FINE LACE
SO NICE AND COOL
THAT IS THE RULE

WORLD AFLAME

WORLD AFLAME
WHO TO BLAME
MASSIVE GRAVES
PEOPLE ARE SLAVES
YOU SIT BY
WONDER WHY
SO YOU THINK
ON THE BRINK
SPIRIT LIVES
SO LOVE GIVES
HUMAN HEART
SOON WILL START
WHO TO BLAME
WORLD AFLAME

WORLD CHANGING

WORLD CHANGING
STOP DERANGING
THIS IN MIND
YOU WILL FIND
PEOPLE AWAKE
FOR YOUR SAKE
TAKE A STAND
IT'S YOUR LAND
GROW YOUR FOOD
CHANGE YOUR MOOD
DO IT NOW
WORK THE PLOW
STOP DERANGING
WORLD CHANGING

WORLD CHAINS

BREAK THE CHAINS
END YOUR PAINS
SPEAK YOUR WORD
MAKE IT HEARD
TELL YOUR FRIEND
MAKE IT END
DO IT NOW
FIND OUT HOW
USE YOUR MIND
THERE YOU FIND
ANSWERS NEW
INSIDE OF YOU
END YOUR PAINS
BREAK THE CHAINS

WORLD CONTROLLED

WORLD CONTROLLED
LOVE UNFOLD
ALL ARE SLAVES
SLEEPING KNAVES
NEVER WAKE
FOR THEIR SAKE
TILL NO FOOD
CHANGE THE MOOD
WORK THE LAND
USE YOUR HAND
THEN YOU EAT
NO DEFEAT
WORLD CONTROLLED
LOVE UNFOLD

WORRY

DO YOU WORRY
LIVE IN HURRY
YOU GO FASTER
FIND DISASTER
COOL DOWN MY FRIEND
THERE IS NO END
FOR THINGS TO DO
THAT CONTROL YOU
YOU LOOK AND LOOK
READ A NEW BOOK
ANSWER YOU FIND
TRY TO UNWIND
THEN YOU FIND OUT
WITHOUT A DOUBT
FALSE IS THE GAME
THERE IS NO SHAME
SO WHY WORRY
LIVE IN HURRY

Y

TO BREATHE
TO EAT
TO SLEEP
TO LOVE AGAIN
YOU ARE EVERYTHING

YOU ARE EVERYTHING

YOU ARE EVERYTHING
YOU DON'T HAVE TO BECOME ANYTHING
YOU DON'T HAVE TO DO ANYTHING
YOU ARE EVERYTHING
FROM THE DAY YOU ARE BORN
THEY HAVE PLANS FOR YOU
AND THEN YOU HAVE PLANS FOR YOURSELF
SO YOU STRUGGLE AND WORK
HARDER AND HARDER
AND YOU BEGIN TO ACQUIRE
DRIVEN BY YOUR FIRE
AND THEN YOU HAVE
AND THEN YOU GET MORE
AND THEN YOU WANT MORE
AND EVEN MORE
AND THEN YOU THINK
DO I HAVE ENOUGH
AND WHEN YOU DECIDE YOU DO
IF YOU ARE HEALTHY ENOUGH
YOU STOP AND SIT
AND SEE NATURE
THEN YOU LOOK BACK
AND YOU WAKE UP
AND WONDER WHAT FOR
YOU'VE REACHED THE DOOR
YOU ARE AWARE
YOU SEE CLEARLY NOW
AND RELAX
YOU DON'T HAVE TO BE ANYTHING
YOU DON'T HAVE TO DO ANYTHING
YOU ARE EVERYTHING
YOU JUST NEED TO LOVE

YOU ARE HOME

YOU ARE HOME
NEED NOT ROAM
LOOK AROUND
HEAR THE SOUND
NATURE'S VOICE
SO REJOICE
LOOK INSIDE
KNOW YOUR PRIDE
LEARN THE WAY
EACH NEW DAY
SO YOU FIND
YOUR OWN MIND
NO NEED TO ROAM
YOU ARE HOME

YOUNG

YOU'RE YOUNG AND STRONG
LAST ALL NIGHT LONG
OH THOSE STRONG SIGHS
CURVES OF THOSE THIGHS
LOOKED IN THOSE EYES
THOUGHT YOU WERE WISE
TO YOUR SURPRISE
IT WAS ALL LIES
YOUR ILLUSION
YOUR CONFUSION
NOW YOU REALIZE
ALL THOSE FALSE TIES
YOUR DREAMS SHATTERED

YOUR HEART BATTERED
SO WHAT TO DO
STILL LOVING YOU
AND WHERE TO TURN
SO MUCH TO LEARN
AND WHERE TO START
WITH BROKEN HEART
YES IN THOSE DAYS
LEARNED NEW WAYS
SO YOUNG AND STRONG
I LEARNED LIFE'S SONG

YOUR DREAM

GO FIND YOUR DREAM
IT ALL DOES SEEM
AN ILLUSION
A DELUSION
YOU RUN AND CHASE
WITH GOD'S GOOD GRACE
WITH ALL YOUR HEART
AND A FAST START
AND AROUND YOU GO
CHASING YOUR TOE
THEN YOU FIND OUT
YOU GIVE A SHOUT
WHAT HAVE I DONE
WHERE IS THE FUN
I WORKED SO HARD
AND ON MY GUARD
I DID MY BEST
I PASSED THE TEST
FOLLOWED THE RULES
LIKE ALL THE FOOLS
THEN I CHANGED
LIFE REARRANGED
THEN I FOUND LOVE
BELOW ABOVE
ANOTHER DREAM
IT ALL DOES SEEM

YOUR DREAM (2)

SO LIVE YOUR DREAM
THEN IT WILL SEEM
TO BE SO REAL
ILLUSIONS STEAL
AND THERE YOU FIND
A DIFFERENT KIND
OF INSIDE WORLD
NEW FLAG UNFURLED
SO THEN YOU SEE
ALL THAT CAN BE
NOTHING REFUSED
NO MORE CONFUSED
YOUR DREAM EXPIRES
YOU LIGHT NEW FIRES
THEN IT DOES SEEM
YOU HAVE NEW DREAM

YOUR HEART

WITH LOVE IN YOUR HEART
YOU HAVE A GOOD START
FEELINGS GO SO DEEP
EYES BEGIN TO WEEP
AND THEN YOU REALIZE
YOUR HEART IS SO WISE
FOR ONLY IT KNOWS
THE GREAT WAY IT GOES
YOU LET GO OF PAIN
AND THE WORLD INSANE
WITH LOVE IN YOUR HEART
YOU HAVE A GOOD START

YOUR HEART (2)

OPEN YOUR HEART
GET A NEW START
LET GO OF PAIN
MAKE A NEW GAIN
LOVE COMES IN
YOU WILL WIN
YOU WILL FEEL THE JOY
OF A GIRL OR BOY
WHO HAS NOT BEEN HURT
WHO'S HEART IS ALERT
WHO'S HEART IS ALIVE
WHO'S LOVE CAN STILL THRIVE
LOVE IS LIKE GOOD FOOD
IT CHANGES YOUR MOOD
MAKES YOU FEEL LIKE LIVING
FEELS GOOD TO BE GIVING
SO OPEN YOUR HEART
AND GET A NEW START

YOU KNOW

YOU THINK YOU KNOW
YOUR GAME YOUR SHOW
AND THEN YOU FIND
YOU ARE SO BLIND
THERE'S SO MUCH MORE
BEHIND THE DOOR
OPEN YOUR EYES
TO BECOME WISE
SO YOU CAN LEARN
YOUR HEAD WILL TURN
SO SEE THE REST
AND DO YOUR BEST
NOW IS YOUR CHANCE
A NEW LIFE DANCE
YOUR SHOW YOUR GAME
YOU WERE SO LAME
ONLY YOU TO BLAME
AND THE FALSE FAME!

YOUR HEART CAN TALK

YOUR HEART CAN TALK
SO WALK THE WALK
LOVE HAS A VOICE
IT IS YOUR CHOICE
FEEL IT AND SEND
MAKE YOUR BRAIN BEND
THE OLD THOUGHTS AWAY
START A NEW DAY
SO HEAR YOUR HEART
IT'S VERY SMART
IT KNOWS THE BEST
WILL DO THE REST
SO WALK THE WALK
YOUR HEART CAN TALK

YOUR LIFE

THINK OF YOUR LIFE
IT'S JOY OR STRIFE
YOU CAN DECIDE
YOUR HEART YOUR GUIDE
OR SOME OF EACH
YOUR LIFE WILL TEACH
IT'S HOW YOU THINK
QUICK AS A WINK
THE DAYS GO BY
YOU LAUGH AND SIGH
HOW YOU REACT
THAT IS THE FACT
PEACEFUL AND CALM
EXPLODE LIKE BOMB
LEARN TO CONTROL
BE A GOOD SOUL

WITH LOVE AND PEACE
ANGER DOES CEASE
SO BE AWARE
SHOW THAT YOU CARE
BE A GOOD FRIEND
FROM START TO END
IT'S JOY OR STRIFE
YOU CHOOSE YOU LIFE

YOUR LIFE

WRITE A NEW POEM
FIND A NEW HOME
FREE YOUR OLD MIND
NEW TREASURE FIND
IT'S ALL INSIDE
YOUR INNER GUIDE
GIVE IT A CHANCE
DO THE NEW DANCE
DO WHAT IT TAKES
TAKE OFF THE BRAKES
BE AMAZING
NOT SAME GRAZING
MAKE YOURSELF FREE
AND THEN YOU SEE
YOU'RE CREATIVE
LIKE OLD NATIVE
YOUR LIFE IS YOURS
OPEN THE NEW DOORS
AND SMILE WITH JOY
PLAY YOUR NEW TOY
IT'S ALL YOUR GAME
AND HAVE NO SHAME
FREE YOUR OLD MIND
NEW TREASURE FIND

YOUR LIFE (2)

IF YOU ONLY KNEW
HOW THEY TURN THE SCREW
AND YOUR MIND WAS AWAKE
JUST FOR YOUR OWN SAKE
YOU COULD HELP YOUR FRIENDS
ACHIEVE BETTER ENDS
IF YOU TAKE THE TIME
UNDERSTAND THIS RHYME
THEN PLEASE LET ME KNOW
THE WAY YOU WILL GO

YOUR MIND

WHO OWNS YOUR MIND
THERE YOU WILL FIND
THEY WILL CONTROL
YOUR VERY SOUL
IT'S TIME TO BE
HAPPY AND FREE
SO YOU CAN FIND
YOUR PEACE OF MIND
CRITICAL THOUGHT
NEEDS TO BE TAUGHT
SO START TODAY
MAKE IT YOUR PLAY
ENJOY YOUR GAME
IT'S ALL THE SAME
THERE YOU WILL FIND
WHO OWNS YOUR MIND

YOUR MIND CONTROLLED

YOUR MIND CONTROLLED
MANY LIES UNFOLD
BELIEVE WHAT'S TOLD
THEN WARS ARE SOLD
BECOME ALERT
OR YOU WILL HURT
USE YOUR GOOD MIND
TRUTH YOU WILL FIND
LEARN TO THINK MORE
OPEN THE DOOR
KNOW WHAT THEY DO
TO ENSLAVE YOU
MCDONALD'S COKE
SOON YOU WILL CHOKE
CHEMICALS MORE
DEAD ON THE FLOOR
THERE YOU WILL BE
THEN YOU WILL SEE
MANY LIES UNFOLD
YOUR MIND CONTROLLED

YOUR WAY

EACH DAY LIVE AND PLAY
DO THE THINGS YOUR WAY
AS YOU WATCH THE WORLD
STRANGE THINGS UNFURLED
NATIONS CONQUER NATIONS
SOME LIVE ON RATIONS
SO WATCH WHAT YOU DO
FIND OUT THE NEW YOU
DISCOVER YOURSELF

LISTEN TO YOUR ELF
HIDDEN DEEP INSIDE
SO LEARN TO TAKE PRIDE
DO THE THINGS YOUR WAY
ALL IS GAME TO PLAY

YOUR WAY (2)

YOU MUST FIND YOUR OWN WAY
AND LIVE IT EVERYDAY
THE WORDS OF OTHERS
ARE LIKE BIG MOTHERS
ONLY YOU CAN KNOW
THE WAY YOU MUST GO
NO ONE KNOWS YOUR INSIDE
SO KEEP YOUR HEART AND PRIDE
WHAT'S RIGHT FOR YOU
WILL SEE YOU THROUGH
KEEP YOUR MIND ALERT
AND YOUR EYES WILL FLIRT
WITH ALL THAT IT SEES
THE BULLETS AND BEES
AND YOUR EARS WILL HEAR
YOUR MIND WITHOUT FEAR
THEN YOU'LL KNOW YOUR WAY
LIVING IT EACH DAY

YOUR WORLD

LIVE IN YOUR WORLD
FETUS UNFURLED
THINK YOU KNOW IT
LIKE TO SHOW IT
PLEASE THINK AGAIN
TRAPPED SLAVE IN PEN
PLEASE UNDERSTAND
YOU'RE NOT SO GRAND
JUST SPECKS OF LIGHT

ACTING SO BRIGHT
HOPING TO FIND
SIMILAR KIND
LOOK EVERYWHERE
TRY HERE AND THERE
THEN YOU REALIZE
YOU'RE NOT SO WISE
FIND THE REAL WORLD
FETUS UNCURLED

YOURSELF

GO FIND YOURSELF
YOUR ON A SHELF
AND THERE YOU STAY
EVERY NEW DAY
DO THE SAME THINGS
YOU LOST YOUR WINGS
LONG TIME AGO
WATCHING THE SHOW
THEY MAGNETIZE
YOUR VERY EYES
THEY'VE GOT YOUR EARS
CREATE YOUR FEARS
THEY OWN YOUR BRAIN
YOU'VE BECOME LAME
BUT YOU DEFEND
UNTIL THE END
THEN THERE'S A SHAKE
A BIG EARTHQUAKE
AND THEN YOU FALL
RIGHT OFF THE WALL
NO MORE SHELF
A NEW SELF

YOURSELF

BE YOUR OWN SELF
NOT BOOK ON SHELF
USE YOUR OWN MIND
THERE YOU WILL FIND
WHO YOU CAN BE
AND THEN YOU SEE
YOU'RE A GROUP SLAVE
A KIND OF KNAVE
YOU HAVE GROUP FEAR
YOU HOLD THEM DEAR
THEY ARE YOUR BRAIN
THEY CAUSE YOU PAIN
BECAUSE YOU OBEY
EVERY NEW DAY
SET YOURSELF FREE
LISTEN HEAR ME
COURAGE YOU CAN GROW
YOU THEN WILL KNOW
HOW YOU CAN RISE
AND REACH THE SKIES
AND DREAM YOUR DREAM
THEN LIFE WILL SEEM
NEW PLACE TO LIVE
NOTE EMPTY SIEVE
SO KNOW YOURSELF
DON'T WAIT FOR ELF

LIFE IS GOOD
IN THE WOOD
NO MORE HURRY
SO DON'T WORRY

FORTY TWO YEARS AGO
THIS FACE I DID SHOW
OH WHAT A GREAT CHANGE
MY LIFE REARRANGE
NOW GONE IS MY YOUTH
AND AIN'T THAT THE TRUTH
NOW ALL I CAN SAY
LIVE WITH LOVE EACH DAY

www.worldheartrevolution.com
www.lifestylepsychotherapy.com
doctorwalter123@gmail.com

THE MESSAGE LOOK INSIDE

STOP LOOKING OUTSIDE
YOU ARE WHAT YOU ARE LOOKING FOR
YOU HAVE THE LOVE, YOU ARE THE LOVE
WE TOGETHER ARE THE POWER OF LOVE
WE TOGETHER CLEAN OUT THE OLD WEEDS
WE TOGETHER PLANT THE NEW SEEDS
WE TOGETHER ARE THE PRESENT
WE TOGETHER ARE THE FUTURE
WE ARE TOGETHER WITH THE PLANET
WE THINK WE ARE SEPARATED BY OUR EGOS
WE ARE INCREASING OUR NEW CONSCIOUNESS
WE LOOK AT OURSELVES
WE SEE THE TRUTH
WE SEE THE LIGHT
WE ARE THE LIGHT
WE ARE THE VIBRATIONS OF LOVE